D0850500

# Atheism
## and the Rejection of God

---

### Contemporary Philosophy
### and *The Brothers Karamazov*

VALUES AND PHILOSOPHICAL INQUIRY

*General Editor: D. Z. Phillips*

*Also in this series:*

RIGHTS AND PERSONS

A. I. Melden

# Atheism
# and the Rejection of God

CONTEMPORARY PHILOSOPHY
AND *THE BROTHERS KARAMAZOV*

STEWART R. SUTHERLAND

Basil Blackwell : Oxford

ISBN 0 631 17500 8

Set and printed in Great Britain. This book is the first to be
photoset by Western Printing Services Ltd, Bristol, on their
V.I.P. phototypesetter. The typeface used is 10 on 12 point
Bembo. Printed by offset lithography by William Clowes &
Sons Limited, London, Beccles and Colchester.

# Contents

# Preface

A conviction underlying the study which follows is that the separation of philosophical from literary inquiry is detrimental to both. That there are difficulties in reconciling the one with the other is not in dispute, but of course intellectual inquiry cannot hope to avoid intellectual effort. The book is essentially a study of one form of atheism and the reply to it which Dostoyevsky, who delineated it in words and images, thought possible. None the less, at a subsidiary level it is hoped that some contribution has been made towards defining the problems to be encountered in the attempt to combine philosophical discussion with the interpretation of a literary text.

A further complication in this case has been linguistic, and one's reluctance to discuss a literary text virtually wholly through the medium of translations, was overcome in the light of four considerations. Initially the response from academic colleagues whose expertise lies in the study of Russian, and particularly Dostoyevsky's, writings was encouraging. Secondly Dostoyevsky's novels are available in English translations of high quality and have been so for some considerable time. In addition, the influence of English writers on Dostoyevsky, whose English was, to say the least, sparse, was considerable. Finally, the need for particular academic foundations is dictated by the range of the study and the nature of the conclusions.

The quotations from *The Brothers Karamazov* are, unless otherwise noted, from Constance Garnet's translation. The only variations from this are the few instances in which I have preferred David Magarshack's version. These latter are indicated by the addition of the letter 'M' to the page reference, thus '(p. 78M)'. For the sake of uniformity I have used the spelling 'Dostoyevsky' throughout, except in quotations, article, or book-titles, from authors who have adopted an alternative spelling.

The philosophical account of the notion of 'a form of life' in

Chapter VI is drawn from my paper 'On the Idea of a Form of Life', published in *Religious Studies* Vol. 11, 1975, and I am grateful to the editor for permission to incorporate sections of that article in the present text. The summary of 'The Legend of the Grand Inquisitor' offered in Section I of Chapter V has been used in a rather different context in a lecture published in the *Yale Review*, titled 'Dostoyevsky and the Grand Inquisitor: A Study in Atheism'.

Chapters III and IV of the book were written while I was a Visiting Fellow at the Humanities Research Centre of the Australian National University, and I am grateful to the Centre for the opportunity thus afforded me, and also to the staff of the Philosophy Departments in the School of General Studies and the Research School of Social Sciences for the stimulation of their discussion and interest. Sections of the book have been read as papers to the D Society, University of Cambridge, the British Dostoyevsky Seminar, the Christian Philosophers Group, the Ohio Academy of Religion and the Philosophy Societies of King's College London, the University of St Andrews and the University of Tasmania. I am grateful to the members of these groups for their varying insights and criticisms. Alan Millar, Kim Lycos, and Andrew Noble each provided extremely helpful comments on particular themes and chapters, and I am much indebted to the editor of the series, Professor D. Z. Phillips, for the accuracy with which he pinpointed areas of the text in need of clarification or emendation. At times, however, I have chosen not to defer to objections raised and inevitably the responsibility for what follows must rest with the author alone.

The philosophers, writers, and literary critics to whom I owe my greatest intellectual debt are clearly indicated in the various references and footnotes, but two men in particular helped encourage and clarify my wish to work in the area of overlap between philosophy and literature and it is appropriate that I should acknowledge my debt to them, the late Dr. Ian Forrest of Aberdeen, and Professor Donald MacKinnon of Corpus Christi College, Cambridge.

To Miss Jane Waye and Miss Ann Wilson my thanks are due for the patience and skill exercised in typing and re-typing the manuscript.

My greatest debt, however, is to my wife to whom I dedicate this book.

STEWART R. SUTHERLAND

Dunblane, December 1975

# Introduction

The spirit of sectarianism has been hitherto our fault and the cause of our failures. We have imprisoned our own conceptions by the lines which we have drawn, in order to exclude the conceptions of others. (S. T. Coleridge, *Biographia Literaria*.)

A book which attempts to combine philosophical, religious and literary inquiry requires, alas, if not an apologia, at least an introduction. What is offered in this study is more of a tapestry than a single chain of argument. The limited variety, it is hoped, will find its unity in an underlying concern with the respective natures of atheism and religious belief.

The opening chapter delineates the various forms of atheism generally regarded as proper subjects for discussion in contemporary English-speaking philosophy. While not wishing to reject these patterns of argument, nor to regard them as anything less than sophisticated and important, there does remain a discontent with the adequacy or completeness of these arguments. Yet even here there is to be found evidence of a general point seldom explicitly acknowledged, namely that atheism may take a variety of different forms. The varieties, however, are more diverse than is dreamt of in the pages of many philosophical journals and texts.

A case in point is Ivan Karamazov, widely accepted as being a masterly portrayal of an atheist, yet not, as I have argued in Chapter II, quite fitting the definitions of atheism tacitly adhered to in many philosophical writings. Thus the study of atheism and belief finds its focus in the person of Ivan, exceptional, enigmatic, but very precise in the charges which he lays against the God of Christianity. Through Ivan, Dostoyevsky explored the profundity of at least one form of atheism, and in response to this he outlines a form of religious belief which he regarded as at least a potential alternative to

Ivan. His exposition of both atheism and belief contains all the cogent particularity which gives that characteristic combination of denseness and sharp definition to Dostoyevsky's characters. That *The Brothers Karamazov* must always be treated as a novel and not as a philosophical treatise is not in dispute, but it is a novel which deals in philosophical themes. As such, as I have argued particularly in Chapters III, IV, VI and VIII, it is susceptible of interpretation in philosophical terms in a fashion which is at least a partial measure of its greatness.

Inevitably, however, such detailed discussion of a novel has involved an extension of the study into literary issues normally separated from philosophical discussion by two hard covers and several classification points in the Library of Congress Catalogue. There are no hard and fast borderlines here and although this does increase the temptation to intellectual vagrancy, withdrawal to 'safe' or non-contested areas of inquiry by both philosophers and literary critics has diminished the contribution which each has to make to 'the proper study of mankind'. Where to set the perimeter to one's discussion does become, then, a matter of judgement in which there is room for divergence of opinion, and in which there are no commonly accepted cultural guidelines. This study is the result of an attempt to subdue the academic reticence of one formally trained in only one of these disciplines, while avoiding the dangers of superficiality in either. Nonetheless it has seemed to me necessary at times to labour points which will seem obvious to some potential readers, because they may be largely unfamiliar to others. Doubtless also, there will be some who will reasonably ask why the first chapter of a book which is in part at least a study of *The Brothers Karamazov* hardly mentions either Dostoyevsky or literature, and manages to include the name 'Karamazov' only twice before the last sentence.

The only reply which I can offer is the book which follows. It does attempt to show how philosophy and literature have much to contribute to one another, but it does so by study of a particular novel and a specific philosophical question, rather than by trying to formulate a general statement about Philosophy and Literature. This has meant that many aspects of the novel have not been discussed and that many of the philosophical questions which could arise in a discussion of atheism and belief have had to be left for another occasion.

# I

# Philosophy, Atheism and Belief

... theists assert and atheists deny that there is a Being called God. ...

## 1

Philosophers of religion could profitably spend much more time than they do examining the tissue, bone, and muscle of atheism. If part, at least, of the task of the philosopher is as Cook Wilson outlined it, 'Bringing belief to a consciousness of itself',[1] then the familiar, religious belief, will undoubtedly be seen the more clearly for a period of reflection upon the unfamiliar and converse, atheism. Often a truncated account of what belief can be goes hand in hand with lack of attention to the complexity and subtlety of certain forms of unbelief. Immediately, of course, to speak of the task of philosophy in these terms is to speak in a way which will not be acceptable to many contemporary philosophers, and even less, it seems, to laymen with an interest in the philosophy of religion. Many who look to the philosopher of religion for illumination would be surprised as well as disappointed to be told that what they may expect is that the philosopher will help them 'bring their belief to a consciousness of itself', help them see that belief for what it is. What they expect, and what many philosophers of religion profess to offer, is something much more than this: an account of whether their belief is true or false, well founded or ill founded, and an account of what constitutes, or would constitute, a solid or rational foundation for such beliefs.

It is not proposed here to argue formally against this latter view and for that outlined by Cook Wilson. Others have done that directly and by implication elsewhere.[2] In so far as this essay defends or supports Cook Wilson's view it will be by exemplifying and adopting it, though I should be more than content if at the end of the day it could be said that the essay has carried out *a* rather than *the* task of philosophy here. It is relevant to point out, however, that when a dispute arises about the *nature* or *role* of philosophy in any particular area, it is difficult to see what it would be like, in *general* terms, to show that one view of philosophy and the task of philosophy is right, and another mistaken: it is much more a matter of practising philosophy as one understands it, and critically evaluating the particular results achieved and the particular patterns of argument and inquiry which have been followed.

In this chapter I propose to consider the arguments and conclusions offered by a number of contemporary philosophers on the topic of atheism. Largely these will be philosophers who do seem to view the role of the philosophy of religion in terms of offering a rational justification of, or basis for, atheism or its opposite. In the following chapter I shall consider in some detail the exemplification of atheism found in Ivan Karamazov. The interpretation of Ivan offered there will, in general terms, be seen as an attempt by Dostoyevsky to bring atheism, or at least one form of atheism, to a consciousness of itself. All of this, in turn, will be seen as part of the dialectic of the whole novel, in which Dostoyevsky explored the problem 'which has tormented me consciously or unconsciously all my life — the existence of God'.

## 2

In the writings of philosophers in the English-speaking world not a great deal of space is devoted to discussing atheism. There are, I think, a number of reasons for this and one of the most important of these is the tacit but widespread assumption that there are no great philosophical problems involved in giving an account of what atheism is. The main, even sole issue about atheism, so the unstated premiss seems to run, is whether or not it can be shown to be either true or false. There is no doubt but that this is a crucially important question, but what is not equally free of doubt is the assumption that we can settle this question without a prior and detailed inquiry into the nature of atheism. A corollary of the proposed view, of course, is the assumption that it is quite clear what the believer means when he claims to believe that God exists and that the only remaining question of interest is whether or not this belief is justifiable, or rationally based. There is an internal relation between the account which one gives of atheism and the account which one gives of belief: if the one lacks subtlety so will the other.

In his popular and helpful introductory text, *Philosophy of Religion*, John Hick offers the following definitions:

Beginning at the negative end of the scale, *atheism* (not-Godism) is the belief that there is no God of any kind; and *agnosticism*, which means literally 'not-know-ism', is in this context the belief that we do not have sufficient reason to affirm or to deny God's existence.[3]

These definitions simply formalize, in the context of an introductory text, what few other philosophers bother to state explicitly, but what, along with many non-philosophers, they take to be a clear and adequate account of the situation. It is interesting to note that even those recent books on the philosophy of religion which profess to be offering 'a clarification of concepts',[4] rather than presenting a case for (or against) Christian theism,[5] seldom devote any space to clarifying what atheism is. Rather, such books have tended to presuppose the sort of account of atheism, the bare bones of which are traced out in Hick's definition. Conversely the account given of the opposite of atheism, theistic belief, has had to be such that its denial could be stated as 'the belief that there is no God of any kind'. The reader may feel irritated by this repetition of what seems all so obviously true, but in fact, in due course, it is precisely the truth and adequacy of this nexus of views which will be challenged.

It would be tedious to indicate in detail for the whole range of recent books on the philosophy of religion just where such emphases are to be seen, but there is some obligation upon me to indicate, at least, that they are there in just the form I suggest. For example, in his discussion of God's relation to the world, C. B. Martin writes:

. . . *theists assert and atheists deny that there is a Being* called God who created the world, watches over men, knows their actions, hears their prayers, cares for their needs, speaks in the whirlwind, took upon himself flesh and walked upon earth and was seen and heard and felt.[6]

Or again, in discussing the complexities of what it means to say that religion is rational, McPherson argues:

Traditionally, to hold that religion is rational is not to hold that every detail of it is capable of being established by argument, but rather that *its centre*, which has been generally held to be *the existence of a Supreme Being with a particular set of attributes*, can be so established, as a basis on which revelation, or faith, may then build up the rest.[7]

Or, finally, to draw an arbitrary limit, two further quotations, in each case the opening sentence of a recent book by an American writer:

The purpose of this book is to investigate the reasonableness of believing that there is at least one God;[8]

In this study I set out to investigate the rational justification of belief in the existence of God as He is conceived in the Hebrew–Christian tradition.[9]

Although I do not wish to be drawn into detailed discussion of the issue involved at this point, it is worth making two notes on these latter two quotations.

In the first instance it is not immediately clear from the outset just what 'reasonableness' or 'rationality' amount to in this context. Although a reading of the two books here would not obviously support the claim, it does seem to me that there is a difference between saying that religious belief is *reasonable* belief, and saying that it is *rationally justifiable* belief. If I am not simply playing with words here, the distinction which I have in mind must be made clear, and that is what I hope the discussion of *The Brothers Karamazov* in succeeding chapters will help us to do. The second point is that although Plantinga is right to specify the particular religious tradition within which he is working, this does not, as Flew seems to imply,[10] remove all *fundamental* confusion as to the *nature* of the task in hand. The residual and crucial question remains of whether or not we are asking the appropriate question — even if we *do* specify that we are asking not just whether God exists, but whether the God of Abraham, Isaac, and Jacob exists. To be clear on this point is to be clear about the sorts of issue raised by Norman Malcolm in his probingly titled paper, 'Is it a Religious Belief that "God exists"?' Not to over-anticipate, it is a working assumption of this essay that the significance of this question and some of the central issues relevant to assessing its significance are raised by Dostoyevsky in the novel which we are to examine. Its significance in the present context, the prolegomena to a discussion of atheism, is that it sets the question of whether or not a particular attitude to the proposition 'God exists' is a defining characteristic of atheism. An implication of all the quotations offered in the previous two paragraphs is that *it is*, and that Hick is right to define the atheist as a man who denies that God exists.

Let us turn now to the exposition of the other general assumption about atheism stated earlier, that the philosopher of religion's central interest in atheism is whether or not it is 'rationally justified'. There are three different sorts of consideration which are usually offered to support or attack the view that atheism is a rationally sound position.

3

A

One of the central themes in the discussion of atheism and belief both in philosophy of religion and popular apologetics focuses on the question, 'What evidence is there for or against the existence of God?' Discussion here on both sides reaches abominably low levels at times, epitomized perhaps by the nineteenth-century Christian apologist who argued that the existence of a wise and gracious God who provided for his creatures, was evident from the fact that God had so ordered the world that rivers flowed past most of the places where men choose to build towns and villages. There are, however, examples of argument and counter-argument which show considerably more logical acumen and sophistication than this. I propose to restrict myself largely to one such example, not as well known as it might be, but in some ways illustrative of this approach at its best. The point of my examination will not be to settle the issue one way or the other, to take sides in the dispute, but to illustrate the logic of the argument: to discover what it derives from and what, by implication, it makes of, religious belief.

When one speaks of evidence for the existence of God one is speaking inevitably of basically empirical approaches to natural theology, and very often, more specifically, of some version of the teleological argument for the existence of God. One of the most thorough presentations of a teleological argument is to be found in F. R. Tennant's two-volume *Philosophical Theology*.[11] In restricting myself to Volume II, chapter 4, 'The Empirical Approach to Theism: Cosmic Teleology', I shall do less than justice to the detail of Tennant's theory of knowledge outlined in Volume I, but we shall find in chapter 4 what is central to our present discussion.

Many philosophers have viewed Hume's criticism[12] of the teleological argument as finally devastating in its negative conclusions. This is indeed true of the form of argument which he does attack — an argument *from* design. One of the main prongs of the kind of attack mounted by Hume is that in such an argument it is a *petitioprincipii* to equate the presence of *order* in nature with the presence of *design*. Certainly design presupposes a designer, but order does not, and if we are being empirical, order, not design, is where we must start. Tennant makes no such elementary error. His is an argument *to* design. His argument is empirically based, and he realizes quite well that the presence of design is something *to* which rather than *from* which we argue.

In the chapter under consideration Tennant assembles what seems to be impressive evidence in favour of design, and of the existence of a designer. He refers disparagingly to the

Paleyan type of teleology which relied on particular organic adaptions, any one of which was deemed sufficient to prove a divine artificer.[13]

In addition to being an argument *to* design, Tennant's argument was also a *cumulative* teleological argument. Nor, as Tennant describes it, is the 'wider teleological argument'

. . . comparable with a chain whose strength is precisely that of the weakest link; it is comparable rather with a piece of chain-armour.[14]

In some detail he outlines what he calls five 'fields of fact' which cumulatively call for explanation in terms of a 'divine artificer'. Such an explanation he did not wish to be viewed as metaphysical, but very much of a kind with the sorts of causal explanations offered by a variety of sciences:

All causal knowledge is, in the last resort, but reasonable and postulatory: teleology is therefore a development from science along its own lines, or a continuation, by extrapolation, of the plotted curve which comprehensively describes knowledge. And this is the *apologia* for theism such as professes to be reasonable belief for the guidance of life.[15]

For Tennant the difference between knowledge and belief was one of degree rather than of kind, and this was equally true of the difference between the knowledge of the empirical scientist and the belief of the empirical theist.

The five fields of fact which Tennant presents and which, he hopes, cumulatively establish the need for God as an 'explicative' concept, are as follows.

(i) First and perhaps most original is 'the mutual adaption of thought and things' which he calls 'an epistemological argument for the being of God' (pp. 81–3). Here, in the light of his own epistemological theory, Tennant is asking us to reflect upon the fact that the world is not impervious to the categories with which we are capable of operating. (It is clear that this argument does not bear a contingent relation to one's epistemological theory, and as such it is contentious, but this is not the place to follow that particular hare.)

(ii) Tennant points secondly to the adaptions which one finds in the organic world to the demands of the environment. He insists that rather than destroying the relevance of such an argument, Darwinism, if properly understood, provides supporting evidence for such a view.

Gradualness of construction is in itself no proof of the absence of external design. (p. 84)

Indeed 'teleology on a grander scale' (than, say, Paley's) is strengthened, rather than the reverse, by Darwin's findings.

(iii) In the third place, Tennant draws attention to 'the continuity of apparent purposiveness between the two realms' of the organic and the inorganic: 'the dependence of adaption in the one on the adaptiveness in the other' (pp. 86–9). As before, *one* instance of this on its own, or even the whole field of fact itself, establishes nothing. Nor is this one link in a chain: it is a part of a cumulative argument.

(iv) Tennant moves next to the presence of beauty in our experience of nature. Even if it is argued that beauty is very much in the eye of the beholder, rather than intrinsic to natural phenomena, nonetheless

. . . we must allow to ontal Nature an intrinsic constitution such that minds can make beauty as well as nomic order out of it. (p. 90)

Tennant sees the weakness of those arguments which start from and wholly depend upon the aesthetic appreciation of nature, and he eschews here (p. 91) 'all claim to proof and appeals to alogical probability', but he does see this as an essential part of his 'wider teleology'.

(v) The final appeal Tennant makes is to 'man's moral status and experience' (pp. 93–103). He criticizes concisely a number of moral arguments for the existence of God, including Kant's, and puts forward a much more modest set of claims. These claims stress that men are, in the words of Pringle-Pattison, 'organic to the world'. Granted that this claim has a precise sense, and it seems to be a way of laying stress upon the fact that men are physical beings with a chemical constitution, then some questions must be raised about the sort of explanation which can be given of men's preoccupation with what we can only call *moral* attitudes and beliefs.

Set alongside some recent works in the philosophy of religion, Tennant's writings, their terminology, their forms of expression, and patterns of argument, are bound to seem dated; but as a model for what an adequate statement of an empirical argument for the existence of God should be like, the two volumes of the *Philosophical Theology* are of persisting value. This is not, of course, to say anything of the validity of the arguments. They are, in fact, open to criticism in a number of different ways, two of which I shall outline. On the one hand they can be challenged from within a shared conception of the nature of argument appropriate to the discussion of atheism and belief. C. D. Broad, for example, does precisely this in his article on theism in *The Encyclopedia of Religion and Ethics*. On the other hand, the whole framework of argument adopted can be questioned.

Accepting the pattern of argument followed by Tennant, there are three obvious ways in which counter-argument can be generated. These three approaches are found in most treatments of the argument, but they are particularly clearly presented in the works already mentioned, by Hume and Broad respectively. Initially any empirical approach to theistic belief must reckon not just with a selection of the facts, but with all the facts, and the facts include the misery and suffering one sees in the world: the facts include moral and physical evil. If one hopes God to be loving, omniscient and omnipotent, then the existence of, in particular, physical evil seems to be the fence at which the teleological argument must stumble, if not fall. One can, of course, modify one's conception of the deity, and this has been done,[16] but I do not wish to examine the implications of that here. Ivan Karamazov gives to the problems surrounding the existence of evil an even more radical significance than that implied here, and this will form one of the central themes of the next chapter.

Secondly one can offer to Tennant's specific instances of order, or even fields of fact, detailed objections, and alternative interpretation.

Such detailed argument, however, is less effective against Tennant than it is, for example, against Paley, for Tennant is very guarded indeed over the claims which he makes about the significance of any one *part* of his argument, any one piece, or range of evidence. These detailed criticisms, however, cannot simply be set aside, either in themselves, or in so far as they lay the foundations for the third type of 'same-level' criticism which can be made of Tennant's teleological argument. Tennant lays much insistence upon the fact that his argument is a cumulative argument. Although, he argues, each of the five fields of fact can be explained in terms of non-final causes,

It is rather when these several fields of fact are no longer considered one by one, but as parts of a whole or terms of a continuous series, and when for their dovetailing and interconnectedness if sought, such as mechanical and proximate causation seems to supply, that divine design is forcibly suggested. (p. 104)

As Broad pointed out, however, this form of argument can be constructed in support of the opposite point of view. A cumulative *anti*-theistic argument is possible.

The above arguments and counter-arguments, however, all presuppose a particular account of what the difference is between belief and unbelief, whether the unbelief of atheism, or the unbelief of agnosticism. Primarily, it presupposes that the difference is a difference in attitude to the statement 'God exists'. Furthermore it implies that if the differing attitudes which one may have are to be properly based, then they will be based upon an evaluation of the *evidence* for or against the truth of that statement. In question of these dual claims, three different sorts of general remark can be made. For the moment it is simply a matter of outlining rather than evaluating these remarks — a matter of indicating the present state of argument as a philosophical context for the discussion of *The Brothers Karamazov*.

Initially, and of acute embarrassment for any attempt to argue directly and empirically from natural phenomena to the existence of a divine designer, is the point raised by Hume in the following passage from the fifth Dialogue:

And what say you to the discoveries in anatomy, chemistry, botany? . . . These surely are no objections, replied CLEANTHES: They only discover new instances of art and contrivance. It is still the image of mind reflected on us from innumerable objects. Add, a mind *like the human*, said PHILO. I know of no other, replied CLEANTHES. And the liker the better, insisted PHILO. To be sure, said CLEANTHES.

Now, CLEANTHES, said PHILO, with an air of alacrity and triumph, mark the consequences. *First*, By this method of reasoning, you renounce all claim to infinity in any of the attributes of the Deity.

The teleological argument depends upon assuming a likeness between the divine mind and human minds, and from the point of view of the *strength* of the argument, *'the liker the better'*. If it is to have any cogency as an argument, then the teleological argument is inevitably anthropomorphic. One may, of course, wish to accept this constraint upon one's account of religious belief, but by so doing one eliminates what is, for many, essential to belief in God — belief in the transcendence and otherness of God.

Secondly, a corollary of the above point is that the model of argument adopted makes the question of the existence of God of a logical kind with the question of the existence of, say, the Loch Ness monster. This, it may be argued, is better making it of a logical kind with the question of whether there are fairies at the bottom of my garden, but the gain is more apparent than real. The point is that, just as in the case of the Loch Ness monster, we are now looking for signs or traces of an existent being. If the comparison seems a little over-drawn and fanciful, consider the following question with which Matson begins a 'Review of Conclusions' in his book *The Existence of God*:

Are there any reasons for believing in the existence of a Deity in the sense in which there are or may be reasons for believing in the existence of one's great-great-grandfather, Hengist and Horsa, Himalayan Snowmen . . . ? (p. 239)

Perhaps we may not expect to find conclusive evidence, but we know, or think we know, what sort of evidence would finally settle the argument one way or the other, and as the evidence accumulates, so we move from agnosticism through various stages of atheism or belief as the case may be. The qualms which some feel about this are further clarified by reference to the third sort of difficulty felt with this whole way of arguing. It seems to make God an existent to be located somewhere in the inventory of persons, things and events which comprise what there is. Paul Tillich gave paradoxical but pointed expression to this fear when he wrote:

It is as atheistic to affirm the existence of God as it is to deny it. God is being-itself, not *a* being.[17]

To refer back, this is, of course, the sort of question being raised in Malcolm's 'Is it a Religious Belief that "God Exists"?'

# B

If not every schoolboy, then at least every second-year philosophy undergraduate knows that following the publication of A. J. Ayer's *Language, Truth and Logic*,[18] many of the philosophical questions then under discussion were reformulated. This was true of many questions in the philosophy of religion. For a substantial number of those working in this field, the appropriate treatment of 'the question of the existence of God', to use Dostoyevsky's phrase, was no longer that of Tennant and Broad. The direction which the discussion took, and the ways in which the questions were reformulated, have been charted to saturation point, and a detailed survey is not necessary.[19] The central change, however, has been a move from discussing whether or not God exists, and what evidence we have to assert or to deny this, to the question of whether or not sentences including the word 'God' have meaning or significance. For our purpose it is of some value to distinguish between two themes around which the argument was reformulated.

(i) In the first place, Ayer's position in *Language, Truth and Logic* was that, literally speaking, all utterances about the nature of God are nonsensical. Ayer arrived at this position following the application of the criterion of meaningfulness outlined in the opening chapters of the book, to the language of theology and belief. He argues that either the term 'god' is a metaphysical term, in which case, according to his criterion of meaningfulness, the assertion that 'God exists' 'cannot be either true or false' (p. 115), or,

the sentence 'God exists' entails no more than that certain types of phenomena occur in certain sequences.

In this latter case to speak of the existence of God is to speak *only* of certain regularities in the physical world: that is, it is to accept that statements about God be translated *without remainder* into statements about the physical world. Ayer correctly argues that this is not a view which religious ( = Christian) believers have found acceptable. Furthermore, one of the reasons for the philosopher's interest in what the believer says of his God is quite certainly that the believer has intended much more than, and, as I shall argue, something quite different from, claims about regularities in the physical world.

Ayer's insistence, however, is that to claim to say more than this is inevitably to utter nonsense. On his criterion, utterances about God are meaningless because unverifiable.[20] Reaction to, and application of, some of the trends of the Logical Positivist school was as vigorous within the philosophy of religion as it was, generally, throughout the whole of the range of philosophical discussion upon which it impinged. Ayer had already insisted that his view should not be confused with those traditionally attributed to atheists and agnostics, and in so doing he marked the difference in the nature of the question which was then seen to be at issue between belief and unbelief. Previously, as between Tennant and Broad, there was a commonly accepted view about what the claim 'God exists' meant, and the question at issue was whether or not one believed the claim and whether or not there was telling evidence for or against it. Ayer's view was that the utterance 'God exists' even when negated is nonsensical. The issue between belief and unbelief then became, for many, the issue of whether or not utterances purporting to be about God were meaningful. The counter-suggestions to Ayer were many and varied.[21]

(ii) The second theme relevant to our discussion arose directly from the replies offered by some to Ayer. A number of those who disagreed with Ayer argued that what Ayer had led them to see was not that theological claims were devoid of meaning, but that they were devoid of *factual* content, and by 'factual content' here was meant the sort of empiricist account of fact implied by Ayer and his successors. Ayer suggested the following criterion of a factual statement:

Would any observations be relevant to the determination of its truth or falsehood? (p. 38)

Braithwaite, for example, took the view that religious utterances were not such that any observations would be relevant to their truth or falsehood, and gave an alternative account of the meaning of religious utterances, largely in terms of their ethical significance. In his Inaugural Lecture, *Theology's Central Problem*,[22] John Hick gave expression to a dissatisfaction felt by many with the sort of reply offered by Braithwaite and others, when he wrote of the problem referred to in the title,

... the issue is whether distinctively religious utterances are instances of the cognitive or of the noncognitive uses of language. (p. 1)

In this context it is taken as established that religious utterances do have a meaning, and the issue at stake between belief and unbelief became one of whether or not religious language is cognitive:

Although there are undoubtedly many aspects of religious meaning to which the true–false dichotomy does not apply, it nevertheless remains a question of prime importance whether such sentences as 'God loves mankind' belong to the class of sentences that are either-true-or-false. (Ibid., p. 2.)

On this view the varieties of unbelief include not only those which deny the truth of such claims, but those which offer non-cognitive analyses of them. Although it is of course true that this particular way of formulating the differences between belief and unbelief owes a great deal to developments in philosophy this century, it is not implausible to see the atheism of both Freud and Marx, for example, as implying non-cognitive analyses of religious utterances.

The general features of the sort of discussion outlined in this section which I wish to note are, (1) the centrality given to the question of the meaning of religious language, and (2) the way in which much of the debate surrounding this has been dominated by basically empiricist theories of meaning. If religious language is to be seen as meaningful, then it has been assumed either it is so factually and cognitively (i.e. either it corresponds to some objective reality), or it must be given some analysis in terms of expressing attitudes of the believer. Professor Hick basically tended to adopt the former view,[23] and R. M. Hare, for example, tended to adopt the latter.[24] The concentration on the concept of meaning is indeed much to be endorsed, for how is one to know whether a religious claim is true or false unless one knows what it means? What is not equally acceptable are the sorts of analyses of religious belief and unbelief represented here by reference to Hick and Hare, resting, as they do, on a particular account of what it is for any sort of utterance to be meaningful, and on a particular view of what it is for such a statement to be true or false. In the particular case in question, the claim that God loves us, if it is to be meaningful *and* either true or false, is so only if the reality of God is understood on the model of, say, the reality of the Loch Ness monster. The view for which I shall argue is that although the differences between certain sorts of atheism and certain sorts of belief *may* be formulated in this way, such an account would by no means be either adequate or comprehensive. The claim that religious language lacks meaning can be made in much more subtle fashion, and in part this is what Ivan Karamazov's atheism amounts to.

## C

The third sort of argument which is sometimes used to discredit belief, and to support an atheistic position, can be loosely characterized as an appeal to specifically logical considerations. It is sometimes argued that whatever may appear to be the case on the surface, when the utterances of the believer are subjected to philosophical analysis, they are found to contain contradictions, or to be less than logically adequate to the role which they purport to play. Although this sort of attack on belief is as old as belief itself, three examples from contemporary philosophical writings will help delineate the area in question.

(i) In his essay 'Can God's Existence be Disproved?',[25] J. N. D. Findlay offers an account of 'an adequate religious object'. He argues that if there is a God who is worthy of worship then he must not be such that his existence is a matter about which there can be debate in the sense of offering evidence for and against it. If that were the case then God's existence would be a contingent matter of fact, whereas Findlay claims that

The Divine existence can only be conceived, in a religiously satisfactory manner, if we also conceive it as something inescapable and necessary, whether for thought or reality.

The trouble with this is that according to Findlay it tries to combine two contradictory features, existence and necessity. On what Findlay calls 'the modern view' of necessity, the characterization of an adequate object of worship offered by Findlay, and endorsed by Anselm in at least one of his versions of the ontological argument,

entails not only that there isn't God, but that Divine Existence is either senseless or impossible.

There are a number of ways in which Findlay's views can be challenged, but I shall simply mention two of these. On the one hand one can challenge what he calls 'the modern view' of necessity, in such a way that one permits the statement 'God exists' to be necessarily true without being either simply tautologous or a reflection of a linguistic convention.[26] Alternatively one could argue that to claim, as Findlay does by implication, that all existential statements must be contingent is to dogmatize about language in an unwarranted fashion. It is to claim that there is only *one* kind of existential statement, whereas Malcolm, for example, argues:

There are as many kinds of existential propositions as there are subjects of discourse.[27]

This raises a number of very complex questions surrounding the notions borrowed from Wittgenstein, of a language-game and of a form of life. These will be discussed in some detail later, in the light of Book VI of the *Broth.. s Karamazov*. It suffices for the moment to note that the sort of atheism being advocated by Findlay rests upon a particular analysis of existential statements.

(ii) A particularly sophisticated version of atheism is sketched by Stuart Hampshire in a paper called 'Identification and Existence'.[28] Hampshire points out that he is not arguing that, for example, the account which one is offering of the nature of God involves a contradiction, nor is he arguing that *as a matter of fact*, nothing actually exists corresponding to this account. Nor alternatively is he claiming that theological propositions are meaningless. An atheist, he allows, could well know what a set of theological propositions meant: part of this would be that he knows the criteria according to which true theological propositions are distinguished from false ones. (A slightly more fashionable way of putting this latter point now, would be to say the atheist knows the internal logic, or depth grammar of religious discourse.)

But he may still believe that no statement of this type about God can be accepted as true, in the last analysis, on the grounds that the conventionally accepted criteria of application attached to the subject-term violate some more general requirements which any such criteria of application should satisfy. (pp. 195–6)

The requirement which he is discussing in this paper is that if anything can properly be said to exist, there must be acceptable conditions of, and criteria for, identification and individuation. That is to say, if an individual is to be considered as something which might, or perhaps does, exist, then there must be conceivable circumstances in which we could pick out the individual in question, and do so unambiguously. On the whole, believers have been either unwilling or unable to specify just what such conditions and criteria would be like in the case of God. If one cannot conceive of such possible conditions and criteria, then one may jettison either belief in God or a particular philosophical position. Again, the point to be noted is the implied account of atheism and belief: that the difference between the two is a difference in attitude to the proposition 'God exists'. Further, the implied analysis of that proposition is such that the reality of God is to be thought of as the reality of a discriminable item in the sum total of things that there are. For some it would be highly dubious whether an atheist who professed this account of the existence of God had understood religious language.

(iii) The third example to which I want briefly to turn attention is Ronald Hepburn's approach to the problem of paradox in religion.[29] Hepburn is there discussing paradoxes which arise within religious belief, as distinct, for example, from the paradoxes which can be formulated about religious belief. That is to say, Hepburn is dealing, in the first instance, with the kind of claim made of Jesus of Nazareth, that he is both God and man, or the claims of Trinitarian theology, that God is One God, and yet he is Three, rather than the sort of paradox about religious belief formulated thus by Bernard Williams:

If, then, the Christian faith is true, it must be partly incomprehensible; but if it is partly incomprehensible it is difficult to see what it is for it to be true.[30]

The problem with paradoxical utterances is that one never seems to know where one is with them. When, if at all, may one speak legitimately in paradoxical language?

When is a contradiction not a *mere* contradiction, but a sublime Paradox, a Mystery? How can we distinguish a viciously muddled confusion of concepts from an excusably stammering attempt to describe what has been glimpsed during some 'raid on the inarticulate', an object too great for our comprehension, but nonetheless real for that?[31]

Although not completely happy with Hepburn's formulation of it, I do agree as to the fundamental nature of this question, and as we shall see in subsequent chapters, what one can make of the 'strange words' of religious belief is a crucially important part of Dostoyevsky's treatment of 'the question of the existence of God'.

Hepburn's suggestions, however, of how we might begin to deal with paradoxical utterances, are not equally agreeable. He does not make the sort of mistake of which Kierkegaard accuses many of the opponents of religious belief: viz. the attempt to *explain* paradox by explaining it away, by dissolving the paradox, and thus turning it into something else. Hepburn is much too sensitive to the mood of religious belief to perpetrate that sort of elementary error. He offers two ways of coping with paradox in religion. Initially he suggests that if the believer can provide an ostensive definition of God, then the fear that paradox is simply a euphemism for 'empty contradiction' can be allayed. Alternatively, if, as Hepburn argues, such an ostensive definition is not available, then perhaps the believer can argue that

If we *were* to abandon all talk of 'God' (paradox-ridden though it is), we should immediately cease to be able to make sense of many things which that concept *does* make sense of. (p. 21)

In view of the sorts of remark made earlier in this chapter it should be clear that the first option here is one which I shall be concerned to reject. It is the sort of possibility criticized in general terms by Hampshire. The second option seems much more congenial, but I should prefer to reformulate the possibility outlined, in the following terms:

If we were to abandon all talk of 'God' (paradox-ridden though it is), we should immediately cease to be able to make *the sense that we do*, of many things.

To reformulate in this fashion is only to indicate a starting point. On the one hand it is still to be established what that sense is, and what is so valuable about it that it should not be lost. On the other, and largely this will be the task of the rest of this book, it will have to be established that there is a viable account of the difference between atheism and belief if we follow this path. My argument will be that there is not simply a viable account, but an account of that difference which has been ignored in much contemporary philosophy.

4

In this chapter I have been concerned to suggest that the topic of atheism is not given the detailed consideration which it deserves in the writings of contemporary philosophers of religion. This, it was claimed, is the result of a belief that not much space is required to give an account of what atheism is: for doesn't everyone know that an atheist is someone who says that God does not exist? Some attention has been paid to a range of arguments which have been offered both for and against atheism and many of these bore out my contention that this is the sort of account of atheism tacitly adopted by many contemporary philosophers. Even those forms of atheism explicitly distinguished from this — for example, that proposed by Ayer (cf. p. 13) — in the end endorse the view that if the claims of the traditional atheist and believer were to be meaningful, then they would be so only if the reality of God were understood on the model of the reality of items and people *in* the empirical world.

It is, however, worth reminding ourselves that the point of the brief survey of these arguments was not to enter directly into them in an attempt to settle the issues at stake. The purpose was rather one of eliciting the presuppositions, implicit or explicit, which they contain about the nature of the differences between belief and unbelief. Apart from the point mentioned above about the nature of the reality of God, and the view that atheism must be a denial either that as a matter of fact such a God does exist, or that such a being could exist who also had the attributes traditionally credited to God, or that it could make sense to say that such a being exists, one other general comment about these various arguments can be offered. A feature of all the examples taken is a tendency stated in extreme form by Matson:

I shall try to conduct this investigation dispassionately and judiciously, as if we were arguing about the existence of the Himalayan Snowman, or the antineutrino.[32]

An interesting and important point here is the slide which takes place in this section of Matson's book from 'rational discussion' to 'dispassionate investigation', and a suggestion that a paradigm of these is an argument about the existence of the Himalayan Snowman.

It is relevant to refer once more to Cook Wilson for an alternative view of the situation. He argues, for example,

That the conception of God can only be realised by us with certain emotions, is not only a very interesting fact but it is an essential characteristic of the conception. (p. 459)

If this is true, then there is some question about the legitimacy of the tendency in the above arguments which is pinpointed in the quotation from Matson. Further, there is a very serious doubt implied about the adequacy of any account of the differences between atheism and belief which leaves this element out of the picture. Also highlighted is the problem, mentioned earlier, of what it is for a discussion to be rational. So often, as Cook Wilson reminds us, what the attempt to argue dispassionately, rationally, amounts to, is the application of a model of rationality devised in one context to other, alien, contexts. The trouble with attempting to provide *the* rational basis for a belief, be it the belief of the atheist, or the belief of the theist, is that by so doing we may be essentially altering the character of the belief in question. We transform it into something which it was not. The convictions here tend to be producing the arguments rather than the other way round. Cook Wilson's alternative advice is that

our first business must be to examine into the nature of the basis which the thing or belief is supposed to have already and before our investigation. (p. 446)

My charge is that the arguments which we have been considering in this chapter have conspicuously deviated from the pattern of inquiry laid down by Wilson.

This is, of course, not to imply anything so foolish as the worthlessness of the writings in question. Individually they all, in different ways and to different degrees, indicate possible forms which atheism may take, as by implication do they indicate different forms which belief may take. For example, I find particularly impressive and important the tension to which Hampshire points when he talks of someone in the position of finding that he must either jettison a particular philosophical position, or a particular religious belief. I do not, however (nor, I think, does Hampshire), take it as self-evident that to be consistent, or rational, or to retain one's integrity, will inevitably involve dropping the belief. Philosophical positions as well as religious beliefs can be misguided. Nor is it any part of my argument to deny that the forms of belief and unbelief which lie behind the arguments outlined in this chapter, are in fact adequate characterizations of what, for some, the acceptance or rejection of religious belief amounts to. What I do wish to deny is that the difference between belief and unbelief *must* be characterized in this way: that 'at the end of the day', or 'in the last analysis', the difference between atheism and belief is a difference in attitude to the proposition 'God exists', or a disagreement about evidence for or against the truth or falsehood of this proposition. Atheism and belief can, respectively, amount to much more than this, and to something quite different. It is an evaluation which I should be prepared to defend, that they can also amount to something much more profound than the characterization of them implied by most of the philosophical writings at which we have looked. This is especially true of the atheism of Ivan Karamazov, to whom we now turn.

## NOTES

[1] *Statement and Inference*, vol. ii, pp. 565 ff. The relevant section is reprinted under the title 'The Existence of God', in *Historical Selections in the Philosophy of Religion*, ed. Ninian Smart (S.C.M., 1962), cf. p. 452.

[2] Cf. Cook Wilson, op. cit., L. Wittgenstein, in *Lectures and Conversations* (Blackwell, 1966), ed. C. Barrett, pp. 53–72, and D. Z. Phillips, *The Concept of Prayer* (Routledge & Kegan Paul, 1965), ch. 1.

[3] Op. cit. (Prentice-Hall, 1963), p. 4.

[4] Cf., for example, T. McPherson, *The Philosophy of Religion* (Van Nostrand, 1965).

[5] Cf., for example, A. Flew, *God and Philosophy* (Hutchinson, 1966).

[6] *Religious Belief* (Cornell, 1959), p. 4.

[7] Op. cit., p. 22.

[8] W. I. Matson, *The Existence of God* (Cornell, 1965).

[9] A. Plantinga, *God and Other Minds* (Cornell, 1967).

[10] Cf. op. cit. 1.11–1.14, and 2.2.

[11] Cambridge University Press, reprinted 1968.

[12] Cf. David Hume, *Dialogues Concerning Natural Religion*, ed. N. Kemp Smith (Nelson, 1947).

[13] Op. cit., vol. ii, p. 85.

[14] Ibid., p. 104.

[15] Ibid., p. 120.

[16] Cf., for example, John Stuart Mill's *Nature and Utility of Religion*, where he takes up a dualist stance, arguing that God is not to be conceived of as omnipotent.

[17] *Systematic Theology*, vol. i (Nisbet, 1953), p. 263.

[18] Gollancz, 1936. References to the second edition, 1946.

[19] Two particularly clear and helpful accounts are to be found in F. Ferré, *Language, Logic and God* (Eyre & Spottiswoode, 1962) and R. S. Heimbeck, *Theology and Meaning* (George Allen & Unwin, 1969).

[20] It is, of course, almost a matter of intellectual reflex to add that the principle of verification ran into severe logical difficulties, but for present purposes nothing would be either gained or lost if we were to replace 'unverifiable' by its philosophical successor 'unfalsifiable'. For an introduction to some of the issues here, see J. O. Urmson, *Philosophical Analysis* (Oxford, Clarendon Press, 1956).

[21] In addition to the books mentioned above, see, for example, T. R. Miles, *Religion and the Scientific Outlook* (George Allen & Unwin, 1959); Flew and MacIntyre (eds.), *New Essays in Philosophical Theology* (S.C.M., 1955), ch. VI, 'Theology and Falsification', Flew, Hare, Mitchell and Crombie, and ch. VII, 'Religion as the Inexpressible', T. McPherson; and R. B. Braithwaite, *An Empiricist's View of the Nature of Religious Belief* (C.U.P., 1955).

[22] Delivered 31 October 1967, published by the University of Birmingham.

[23] Cf., for example, his use of the notion of eschatological verification: see 'Theology and Verification', in *The Existence of God*, ed. Hick (Collier-Macmillan, 1964).

[24] Cf. his use of the notion of a *blik* in the essay cited in *New Essays in Philosophical Theology*.

[25] First published in *Mind*, vol. lvii, 1948, reprinted in various places, including *The Ontological Argument*, ed. A. Plantinga (Macmillan Papermac).

[26] Cf., for example, A. Kenny, 'Necessary Being', in *Sophia* I.3, and 'God and Necessity', in *British Analytic Philosophy*, eds. B. A. O. Williams and A. Montefiore (Routledge & Kegan Paul, 1966).

[27] From 'Anselm's Ontological Arguments', originally published

in *The Philosophical Review*, vol. lxix, 1960, reprinted in the Plantinga collection: this quotation from p. 150 of the latter.

[28] Published in *Contemporary British Philosophy*, Third Series, ed. H. D. Lewis (George Allen & Unwin, 1956).

[29] Cf. *Christianity and Paradox*, by R. W. Hepburn (Watts, 1958).

[30] Cf. 'Tertullian's Paradox', reprinted in *New Essays in Philosophical Theology*: this quotation from p. 211.

[31] Hepburn, op. cit., p. 17.

[32] Op. cit., Introduction, p. xi. To be fair to Matson, it is clear that he sees this as perhaps an ideal towards which one approximates, as the subject matter allows.

# II

# Ivan Karamazov and Atheism

Even in Europe there have never been atheistic expressions of such power.

In books V and VI of the *Brothers Karamazov* Dostoyevsky set out

to depict the extreme of blasphemy and the core of the destructive ideas of our age, in Russia, among young people who are divorced from reality— and along with the blasphemy and anarchism, the refutation of them, which I am now preparing in the last words of the dying elder Zossima. . . .[1]

Elsewhere his tone is less prophetic, but he insists that in Book V he is offering a statement of what atheism is through the words of Ivan. At first sight, however, we are confronted with a paradox.

Ivan Karamazov is widely accepted as being a masterly portrayal of an atheist. Yet there is a problem here. On the face of it he seems to be an odd kind of atheist. He advises his brother Alyosha never to think about problems 'which are not of this world', and therefore beyond our intellectual capacities,

especially about God, whether He exists or not (p. 240).

In itself, this injunction would not be particularly remarkable, for indifference, if that be what it is, is a kind of atheism: Ivan, however, goes on to remark and to remark repeatedly,

I accept God.

In essence this is the problem — an atheist who 'accepts God'. Yet so often as we have seen we are told that the difference between belief and disbelief, between atheism and Christianity, is that the believer is primarily one who believes that God exists, and that the atheist is primarily one who believes that God does not exist. We need only remind ourselves of the quotation from Hick:

. . . *atheism* (not-Godism) is the belief that there is no God of any kind; and *agnosticism*, which means literally 'not-know-ism', is in this context the belief that we do not have sufficient reason either to affirm or to deny God's existence.

The problem with this account is that it does not include Ivan Karamazov.

In what follows, I write under the conviction that in offering Ivan as an example of atheism, Dostoyevsky was neither naively mistaken nor philosophically confused. On the contrary, I shall argue that there is great philosophical sophistication in the account of atheism implied in Dostoyevsky's portrayal of Ivan, and that in *The Brothers Karamazov* the limitations inherent in the accounts of atheism outlined in the previous chapter, receive incisive statement. The point, initially at least, is not whether that account of atheism is wholly misleading: I do not think that it is; but whether it is stunted and potentially intellectually crippling. Dostoyevsky's account of atheism is two-sided: on the one hand he is concerned to reject a particular view of what it is to be an atheist, and also the implied view of the sort of discussion which belief may have with unbelief; on the other hand he is concerned positively to offer an alternative account of both atheism and of the sort of discussion appropriate to 'the problem of the existence of God'.

The setting for Dostoyevsky's exposition of atheism is the confrontation of the two brothers, Ivan and Alyosha, in a pub. There they 'get acquainted', they speak to each other at length for the first time. Immediately Dostoyevsky uses the situation to distinguish his own enterprise from the pub discussions of 'the Russian boys and their professors'; those who in chance encounter, meet and talk (or perhaps 'blether').

Apart from the points made in the novel, Dostoyevsky's own personal distaste for the sorts of discussion he has in mind are made clear in the following extract from *The Diary of a Writer*[2]:

The journey from St. Petersburg to Berlin is a long one, lasting almost forty-eight hours. So I took with me two pamphlets and several newspapers just in case. I say 'just in case' because I always fear being stranded in a crowd of unknown Russians of our intellectual class— anywhere in a train carriage, or a ship, or at some public meeting.

Dostoyevsky emphasizes the distinction by focusing upon three different polarities.

1. The first we have already mentioned: the setting of these two brothers searching for mutual self-understanding, brothers whose

destinies, almost in the manner of Greek tragedy, are being worked out before us, setting their discussion over against that of those who by drifting into this pub rather than that, drift into this discussion rather than that.

2. The second polarity is between the sorts of questions discussed by the Russian boys, as opposed to those to which Ivan feels able to address himself. He asks of them:

> What are they going to talk about while snatching a free moment in a pub? Why about eternal questions: is there a God, is there immortality? (p. 273M.)

Of these issues he warns Alyosha,

> And I advise you never to think about it either my dear Alyosha, especially about God whether He exists or not. All such questions are utterly inappropriate for a mind created with an idea of only three dimensions. (p. 240)

There is a sense in which the above and the many similar remarks to be found in this section of the text may be seen as invoking a criterion of meaningfulness and intelligibility akin to those found in Hume, in parts of Kant, and in the logical positivists of this century. As Kant has shown, there is a sense in which certain disputes are beyond resolution because there *can be* no way of settling them. Because of the way in which the questions at issue are set out, because of the form given to them, no answer is possible. At most these disputes may be dissolved, shown to involve self–contradiction, saying what is, logically speaking, unsayable. Dostoyevsky is here indicating his awareness of this sort of point, and also suggesting in his own way - the emptiness of certain sorts of treatment of 'eternal questions' by the setting to which he consigns them. This latter way of implying emptiness or triviality has, as we shall see later, philosophical significance of its own. In opposition to the attempts of the Russian boys to understand the ways of God, and to justify them to men, Ivan insists,

> I understand nothing, and I don't want to understand anything now. I want to stick to the facts. I made up my mind long ago not to understand. For if I should want to understand something, I'd instantly alter the facts and I've made up my mind to stick to the facts. . . . (p. 285M.)

3. The third polarity here is that which focuses at one extreme upon the speculative or hypothetical nature of certain sorts of treatment of 'the problem of the existence of God'. Alternatively, Ivan tells Alyosha,

What I'm trying to do is to attempt to explain to you as quickly as possible what sort of man I am, what I believe in and what I hope for— that's it, isn't it? (p. 274M.)

Dostoyevsky is not here making the point much loved by certain sorts of clergymen, that a discussion of religious belief should be 'practical' rather than 'theoretical' or 'philosophical' (It is usually very difficult to find out what is meant by this): rather he is engaged upon a philosophical discussion of just what the conceptual issues are in any discussion of 'the problem of the existence of God'. He is rejecting one pattern of discussion which sees the issue between atheism and belief as one of two competing hypotheses about which we might speculate, pro or contra, adding up points in favour and points against, 'while snatching a free moment in the pub'. Whatever the difference between atheist and believer, it is being argued, it is not the difference between two speculative hypotheses which may or may not engage the emotions, may or may not affect the pattern of one's life, affect what, in Ivan's words, one 'lives by'. Again, as we shall see, further significance will be found in this polarity.

In the place of such an account of the discussion of belief and unbelief, Dostoyevsky offers us Ivan, an atheist who accepts God, and Alyosha, the disciple of Zossima. What sense can be made of the claim that Ivan is an atheist?

Ivan 'accepts God', but in the same breath he tells Alyosha,

Yet would you believe it, in the final result I don't accept this world of God's, and although I know that it exists, I don't accept it at all. It's not that I don't accept God, you must understand, it's the world created by Him I don't and cannot accept. (p. 241)

As he phrases it more dramatically later on,

It's not God that I don't accept, Alyosha, only I most respectfully return Him the ticket. (p. 251)

This acceptance of God but rejection of his world is the heart of Ivan's atheism, and it functions at three different levels.

Most obviously Ivan's atheism is to be seen in terms of a moral response to what the believer talks of as God's creation. He spells this out selectively in terms of the suffering of small children, and documents his account by describing a number of instances of extreme and vicious cruelty. These instances, as were many of the details of his novels, as well as, in some cases, the plots themselves, were derived from newspaper reports. A voracious consumer of newspapers, in *The Diary of a Writer*, Dostoyevsky speaks of

. . . 'real life' . . . more fantastic than any fiction could hope to be.

'What is to be made of this', or 'How are we to understand these happenings?' or, 'What is the Christian answer to this? Such questions Ivan rejects out of hand and with them the attempts of the Russian boys and their professors to produce a theodicy which can somehow make such suffering intelligible by reconciling it with a loving creator in terms of some cosmic plan which will offer an eschatological solution to, or recompense for, the suffering of the innocent. He sets aside as hopelessly and wholly inadequate, the response to the sufferings of children which leads to acceptance of, or even worse, debate about, a theory or hypothesis. The theories thus spun, he argues, are only countenanced at the expense of 'the facts', at the expense of moral blindness, the dulling of the moral sense. These theories try to make comprehensible what is incomprehensible, and they do so at the price of 'altering the facts'.

Listen: if all have to suffer so as to buy eternal harmony by their suffering, what have the children to do with it — tell me please? It is entirely incomprehensible why they too have to suffer and why they should have to buy harmony by their sufferings. Why should they too be used as dung for someone's future harmony? (p. 286M.)

If Dostoyevsky is concerned to state the case for atheism he does so as incontestably as possible. In a letter to the editor of the journal in which the *Brothers Karamazov* was first serialized, he refers to Ivan's thesis, 'the senselessness of the suffering of children', as 'irresistible'.[3] He accepts, or rather insists, that discussion of the problem of the existence of God cannot be carried on in terms of speculations about the motives or plans of an omnipotent God, who is said to be a God of love, but who seems on the face of it to be quite the reverse.

One response to this sort of argument is to use the facts produced as some kind of evidence for the non-existence of God, making the issue then a matter of hypothesis, evidence, probability, and speculation. This is the use to which such facts are put, for example, by Broad in his attack on Tennant: these are the challenges which, in part, John Stuart Mill's dualism was intended to meet.[4] Ivan, however, has already refused the possibility of such a move:

I have a Euclidean earthly mind, and how could I solve problems that are not of this world? (p. 240)

Speculative atheism is no better than speculative theism. Although he puts the point here in seemingly epistemological terms, this is, in one sense, a preparing of the ground for the second level of his attack on Christianity. His protest, as we have seen from earlier quotations, is essentially in the name of *morality*. Paul Helm makes a relevant point here, when he distinguishes between viewing the existence of evil as an epistemological problem, and viewing it as a moral problem:

For someone who asks, 'Why does God allow the innocent to suffer?' or, 'Why is there so much misery in the world?' the . . . answer, 'I agree, this is a difficulty, but this is because of the nature of religious truth', could not be given. An answer in terms of the mode of apprehension of religious truth would be out of place.'[5]

Ivan, however, rejects not only the sort of epistemological solution to the question of evil offered, for example by Smart,[6] he is also rejecting what Helm allows as at least a possibility, that there could be an adequate theodicy.

Ivan's response to the realities of suffering is instead, as we have noted, to distinguish between God and his creation. To some this will appear rather quaint, particularly in so far as it treats the concept of God in rather anthropomorphic terms. This was the reaction in certain quarters as Book V was published— *The Brothers Karamazov*, as most of Dostoyevsky's other novels, was originally published in serial form in *The Russian Messenger*— and Dostoyevsky complained to a friend,

The villains teased me for my ignorance and a retrograde faith in God. These blockheads did not dream of such a powerful negation of God as that put in the [mouth of the Grand] Inquisitor. . . . Even in Europe there have never been atheistic expressions of such power.[7]

It is at this point that we must probe to the second level of Ivan's atheism.

Ivan's response is that of rebellion, though he has not at this stage seen it in this light; it is Alyosha who first gives this account. Ivan's reply, significant in the light of what is to come, is:

Rebellion? I am sorry to hear you call it that. . . . One can hardly live in rebellion, and I want to live. (p. 252)

Initially, however, the important point is what such rebellion entails. The first strand of Ivan's atheism is rebellion, 'returning the ticket'. The second strand is only seen in the implications of this rebellion.

Ivan has chosen rebellion as his response to suffering, but in so doing he has also chosen to 'accept God'; but the God whom he accepts is a false God, the God of the Russian boys, a God whom man has invented (p. 274) and in whose creation a future recompense, a future harmony is preceded by the suffering of the innocent. This is the God about whom man speculates, the God about whose existence or non-existence the Russian Boys talk, 'while snatching a free moment in a pub'. Ivan, however, is not being naive, he is not laying himself open to the charge of self-contradiction, nor to the cry of the believer, 'But you don't understand, that is not the God of worship.' Ivan knows this full well. He deliberately accepts a false God, thereby giving his atheism its most pointed statement.

This, as Dostoyevsky claims, is a denial of God not even dreamt of by those who see only naivety in the novel. In his acceptance of God, Ivan is not going *so* far along the way with the believer, not saying, 'Well we agree at least that God exists, but after this we diverge': he is in fact accepting and projecting the trivialization of the concept of God. He jests with Alyosha by setting a puppet-god upon the throne in a way reminiscent of the fashion in which the apocryphal story tells of Edward I bringing to the people of Wales a Prince who 'cannot speak a word of English' — his newborn son. But Ivan's humour is darker than Edward's for he knows that from the Russian boys and their professors there will be no cry of rage, no sense of being mocked.

Throughout Volume I, Dostoyevsky has left a trail pointing to the grimness, and sometimes inscrutability of Ivan's humour, though in the early stages at least, there is more than a hint that in mocking others Ivan sometimes mocks himself. There is, for example, Ivan's article on the subject of ecclesiastical courts, which met with such mixed reception. The article evoked agreement from both churchmen and atheists, while there were those 'sagacious persons' who opined that the article was nothing but an impudent satirical burlesque (p. 11).

Then there is the important dialogue between Ivan and Zossima, following the first statement, by Miusov, of Ivan's published view that if there were no belief in God or immortality, then 'everything would be permitted'. Referring to the article in which this was advanced, Ivan insists, with a blush,

I wasn't altogether joking (p. 66).

Zossima's diagnosis of this will repay careful consideration, for it contains much that is important in the attempt to understand Ivan:

You were not altogether joking — that's true. You still can't find the right answer to this question (of what could happen if people lost their faith in the immortality of the soul) and you're very worried about it. But even a martyr sometimes likes to amuse himself with his despair, just out of despair. You, too, in your despair, are for the time being amusing yourself with magazine articles and discussions in society without believing in your arguments, smiling bitterly at them with an ache in your heart. . . . But you have not made up your mind what answer to give to that question and therein lies your great grief, for the question urgently demands an answer. (p. 78M.)

Finally, even in the discussion with Alyosha which includes the tale of the Grand Inquisitor, there is that curious mixture of conviction and yet pushing that conviction to arm's length by laughing at it:

Ivan stopped. He was carried away as he talked, and spoke with excitement; when he had finished, he suddenly smiled. (p. 268)

When Alyosha sorrowfully identifies Ivan with the Grand Inquisitor, Ivan disowns the tale — 'a lot of nonsense'. And yet it is clear that this explication of his views to Alyosha, however much he retreats to trivializing its importance, represents a hardening of those views in Ivan's heart and mind. 'We've got everything thrashed out,' he says to Alyosha, though this is not completely true.

Throughout the first five books of the novel, the questions which preoccupy Ivan wring from him, almost against his own intentions, an answer. His humour grows darker as his attitudes harden. There are two points to note here: one is the connection made explicitly by Zossima, and implicitly by Dostoyevsky, between the form which Ivan's humour takes, his emotional responses to the questions which torment him and the role which his humour plays in enabling him to cope with his emotions. The second, and more general point, is the transposition of Cook Wilson's view that it is an essential characteristic of the conception of God that it can only be realized by us with certain emotions.[8] Ivan's atheism is such that it cannot be understood if the role of his emotions, and indeed of his humour, is ignored.

Ivan has 'amused' himself with the question of whether the end of belief in God and in immortality means that 'everything is permitted'. This same grimness of humour, masking intensity of emotion, is seen in his 'acceptance of God'. At one level he laughs at the Russian boys, at another he is well aware that compared with his 'acceptance' of God, the atheism which sees God as improbable hypothesis or as unacceptable axiom is a spineless affair indeed. The *mood* of his denial of God is analogous to his father's practice of bringing home prostitutes and allowing them to usurp his wife's place during a series of wild parties. In religious terms it is to be seen as a breaking of the first two commandments of the Decalogue.

As a footnote to this point, as well as a preparation for the next, it is worth noticing that if the interpretation which I offer of Ivan is legitimate, then a difficulty on which George Steiner makes some tentative comments may be seen in a clearer light. Discussing the role of the concept of God in Ivan's tale of the Grand Inquisitor, and the problem of whether or not the Inquisitor is an atheist, he quotes what he calls a 'gnomic passage' from one of the drafts of this section:

Euclid's geometry. That is why I shall accept God, all the more as it is the everlasting old God and one cannot resolve Him (or make Him out). Let Him be the good Lord. It is more shameful that way.[9]

The ambiguity which Steiner finds here is that which we have been discussing. Steiner suggests,

This appears to signify that the speaker — Ivan or the Inquisitor — is prepared to accept the existence of some kind of ineffectual and incomprehensible deity, if only because this existence would make the state of the world yet more bewildering and outrageous. (Ibid.)

Much more firmly than this, I have been arguing that Ivan's 'acceptance of God' is based on his utter revulsion not just of the arguments of the Russian boys but of the God whom these arguments are intended to persuade us to accept or deny. His acceptance of their God, whom he believes also to be the God of the orthodox believer, is from one respect to be seen as the bitter joke of a man whose moral outrage at the implications of such forms of belief and disbelief is intense to the point of distraction. His atheism is, in its acceptance of 'some kind of ineffectual and incomprehensible deity', profoundly and intentionally blasphemous. To say this is simply to insist upon what is essential to *understanding* Ivan's atheism: it is *not*, as such, to *evaluate* it religiously.

The third level of Ivan's atheism can be seen in what Camus calls his 'even if'. Camus writes as follows:

> Ivan explicitly rejects mystery, and, consequently, God, as the fountainhead of love. . . .
> . . . Ivan rejects the profound relationship, introduced by Christianity, between suffering and truth. Ivan's most profound utterance, the one which opens the deepest chasms beneath the rebel's feet is his *even if*; 'I would persist in my indignation even if I were wrong'. . . . Ivan incarnates the refusal of salvation. Faith leads to immortal life, but faith presumes the acceptance of the mystery of evil and resignation to injustice.[10]

I do not fully accept Camus's interpretation of this point, though I agree that it is crucial. I should prefer to put it in this way. Ivan is not just content to trivialize the concept of God. He is insisting that there is no alternative. He is not simply playing the role of the satirist who shows the believer what his belief can and sometimes does look like. He deliberately accepts a false and inadequate God, and yet there is the problem of Zossima and Alyosha, Zossima whose hand he kisses, Alyosha, the brother for whom he has an obvious affection. They do not quite fit into the pattern of belief which he has outlined and 'accepted', and the risk that there is another possibility, another form which belief might take, has to be denied.

The first strand of Ivan's atheism is rebellion against a God who allows the suffering of innocent children. He argues in this third strand not only that he can see no purpose in this, that it is *senseless* suffering; he further insists that *even if* the wounds were in the end healed and forgotten, and harmony did result,

> I would rather remain with my unavenged suffering and unsatisfied indignation even *if I were wrong*. Besides, too high a price is asked for harmony; it's beyond our means to pay so much to enter on it (p. 251).

This is not rebellion which can be ended, not even by the possibility of salvation. Ivan is not looking for a better deal for these children, for those who suffer. That is not the point of this rebellion. In that sense it is not the rebellion of compassion. No deal could ever compensate for those sufferings. Ivan refuses to view the sufferings as anything other than what they are in themselves. They can *never* be seen as part of a whole, or as means to a 'higher harmony': such is only 'to alter the facts'.

The crux of Ivan's rebellion is that in rejecting God he is rejecting the possibility of *any other* account of belief than that of a 'Euclidean' mind, that which goes hand in hand with trying to make comprehensible what is incomprehensible, trying to make sense of what is ultimately senseless, the suffering of innocent children. In the end of the day, he argues, even the belief of Alyosha and Zossima is of-a-kind-with that of the Russian boys. What this amounts to is a denial that the concept of God and the various concepts which go with it, eternal life, miracle, immortality, and so on, can play any other role than the role which they play in the bar-room discussion of the Russian boys and their professors. He is denying that there can be established any other links between those concepts than those which consign the existence of God to speculation and hypothesis. At the same time, as particularly Book VI of the novel makes plain, he is also denying either validity or intelligibility to a way of life in which the practice of prayer and worship can play a significant and meaningful part — meaningful also in the sense that they indicate a logical role or life for such concepts as God, immortality, miracle, eternal life, other than the role which they have in the patterns of discussion laid down by the Russian boys.

A philosophical coda from Norman Kemp Smith's paper 'Is Divine Existence Credible?'[11] may help to make plain the subtlety of Ivan's atheism at this point. At the outset of his paper, Kemp Smith raises the question of why it is that for so many people religious belief is no longer an option:

Why is it that what was, at least, an open question for David Hume, is for so many no longer worthy of even debate?

His paper then discusses some misunderstandings which may well lie behind this foreshortening of options.

He writes:

The first and main type of misunderstanding I should trace to the fact that those who are of this way of thinking, however they may have thrown over the religious beliefs of the communities in which they have been nurtured, still continue to be influenced by the phraseology of religious devotion — a phraseology which, in its endeavour to be concrete and universally intelligible, is at little pains to guard against the misunderstandings to which it may so easily give rise. As they insist upon, and even exaggerate the merely literal meaning of this phraseology, the God in whom they have ceased to believe is a Being whom they picture in an utterly anthropomorphic fashion. . . . Such a Being could not be otherwise than abashed before the immensities of space and time for which, as Divine, he has to be conceived as responsible. For whatever the honorific attributes assigned to him, he is in essentials finite; and as Hume has so convincingly argued in his Dialogues— in Philo's reply to Cleanthes — a limited and finite God can meet the needs neither of religion nor of theology.

It is instructive to reconsider the three levels of Ivan's atheism in the light of Kemp Smith's suggestion of a connection between the conception of a finite God, the uncritical use of anthropomorphic language, and the detachment of that language from the life of belief and worship in which it has its home.

The God whom Ivan accepts is a finite God, he is the god who is the invention of a Euclidean mind, and of whom one *can only* think and talk in anthropomorphic terms. The setting for such a conception, the context which indicates what can be said of such a god, is the speculations of the Russian boys passing the time of day over a pint of beer. As such it is a setting in which the language of belief is quite detached from the life of the believer. It is in this sense that Ivan is quite happy to accept God: Why not, for what hangs on it? It is in this sense too that he mocks both Alyosha and the Russian boys, for to thus accept God is to trivialize him. At the third level of Ivan's atheism he is not simply mocking Alyosha: he is rather denying that the life to which such language belongs is in any sense a coherent or intelligible possibility. He is denying validity to the life led by Zossima, and in so doing denying that the language belonging to that life, the language which speaks of God, of eternity, or immortality and miracle, can have any role other than that found in speculative discussion. Evidence further supporting this interpretation of Ivan's atheism can be found in the manner in which Dostoyevsky set about answering in Book VI 'all those atheistical propositions', but that must wait for a later chapter.

What I hope has been established in this chapter is the subtlety of Dostoyevsky's conception of atheism, and by implication the need for a much more complex definition than 'Atheism — the belief that there is no God of any kind'. This definition, as we saw in the previous chapter, summarizes the account of atheism presupposed in a great deal of contemporary discussion. Consequently acknowledgement of Ivan as an atheist must put a question mark alongside such discussion. To do so, is not, of course, to doubt the logical sophistication of much of the work which was briefly reviewed: nor is it to deny that much can be learned from a close study of the arguments in question. Nor, furthermore, is it to reject out of hand the accounts of belief and unbelief implied therein. For some, such is what belief and unbelief amount to. Initially and most importantly, the question put to much contemporary discussion of belief and unbelief by philosophers in the English–speaking world, is the question as to the tacitly assumed *comprehensiveness* of their inquiries and presuppositions.

To see that inevitably such discussion will leave out of account the atheism of Ivan, is to see something of what such discussion is: it is, in part, to see the implied accounts of belief and unbelief for what they are, by seeing what their limits are. Thus we have, in one way, been adopting and following Cook Wilson's view of the role of philosophy, trying partially to see certain patterns of argument for what they are. In a more direct way we have seen Dostoyevsky bringing a particular form of unbelief to a consciousness of itself. Of especial importance here is what this implies about the differences which there are between belief and unbelief, and about what sort of dialogue the two may carry on, the one with the other. It is radically different from the sort of argument which one finds between Broad and Tennant, between Hare and Flew, or between Hick and Braithwaite, and its difference from these is essentially a difference in conceptions of the reality of God, a difference in accounts of what it may mean to assert or deny that reality.

In attaching philosophical significance to Ivan's atheism, one is not suggesting an *intellectual* parallel between the pub discussions of the Russian boys, or any other pub discussions for that matter, and the sorts of arguments mentioned in the previous chapter. It is, however, to raise a fundamental question about the *significance* of these arguments, and precisely what they are intended to achieve. The parallel goes at least as far as suggesting that these arguments may well have less significance for a philosophical account of religious belief than their authors think or intend them to have: this for a number of reasons which can be elicited from what we know of Ivan.

Basically, as has already been noted, a study of Ivan Karamazov puts a crucial question about the importance attached to the proposition 'God exists' in the implied accounts of the difference between belief and unbelief. What is at stake here is the conception of the reality of God, not just the question of whether there is such a reality, but of what it amounts to, to talk of, and believe in or rebel against, the reality of God. It has already been noticed that Ivan's atheism makes plain that certain forms of belief and unbelief cannot be characterized without reference to the role of the emotions. The trouble is that if the anti-religious arguments in Chapter I turned out to be invalid, and if a parallel set of pro-religious arguments turned out to be valid, one could still quite reasonably say, 'So what?' it need not affect what, as Ivan puts it,[6] 'one lives by'. The conception of God is such that, according to the pattern of argument in question, one could arrive at the belief that God exists without either loving or hating that God, fearing or worshipping him. It is at this point that many believers, and, as we have seen, some atheists, would want to protest, to insist that we are no longer speaking of the God whom they worship or reject.[12] Such an account of religious belief and unbelief, they would argue, must be inadequate. Someone who would rest content with such an account has not understood what belief and unbelief amount to.

For Dostoyevsky, the difference between belief and unbelief is, in a way that is superficially similar to Ayer, a matter of intelligibility and meaning. There, however, the similarity ends. Ayer's proposed solution to the question of whether or not a proposition is meaningful is appeal to the criterion of meaning developed in *Language Truth and Logic*. Ivan and Dostoyevsky have a much more complex conception of meaning. In the first case Ivan clearly sees that the meaning which a whole range of expressions may have depends upon the significance which they can have in the lives of men. If one did accept verificationist or falsificationist theories of meaning then that would raise important questions for the sense which the language of the believer might have. My contention is that it is equally, if not more devastating for religious belief, if the difference between belief and unbelief is essentially a matter for bar-room dispute, is a matter that one can take up or lay down with a pint of beer, 'while snatching a free moment in a pub'. What is at issue here is not a matter of psychology, not a matter of the associations which a number of expressions may or may not have: to argue for that position would again be to assume that the meaning of the language of religion was settled, and that we were dealing solely with the way in which, as a contingent matter of fact, these expressions strike different individuals. What is at issue is the sense which these expressions have, the sense which it makes to say, for example, that God loves men, and the inferences which it is legitimate to draw from this. Prior to this, Dostoyevsky is raising the fundamental question of how we are to discover the sense of a particular range of expressions, and how we are to assess which purported inferences are legitimate and which illegitimate. (On this point he is tackling the issue to which Hepburn points attention: what is to count as a contradiction, and how are we to discover whether a particularly puzzling expression is a contradiction, or whether it is a paradox.) As such Dostoyevsky is engaged, in writing *The Brothers Karamazov*, on a crucially important philosophical task: indeed upon a whole range of philosophical tasks. He is concerned in the first place, as we have seen, to give form to 'the question of the existence of God'. What he sees this as amounting to is giving an adequate characterization of both atheism and belief, and this in turn leads him to the problem of the intelligibility of what the believer says. In the portrayal of Ivan we are given a suggestion which Dostoyevsky is to develop and illustrate in Book VI of the novel, of how it is that we may settle the questions at stake. Ivan sets about trivializing religious belief, by suggesting that the language of religion has as its appropriate home, idle chatter. The role which it can meaningfully play in the life of men is at best that of diversion, more probably that of adding to the flow of the garrulous. Now, there is no doubt that it can play this latter role! The question is, Can it play any other? This, however, the role which a range of expressions can play in the lives of men, is how the question of meaningfulness is to be settled. This is the criterion of whether or not a particular sort of language is meaningful: and it is here, that we must look if we are to find out what meaning these expressions have, if any. In general terms this may sometimes appear to be the sort of programme followed by Braithwaite or Hare, but as we turn to the detail of the inquiry into which Dostoyevsky was led, we shall see that in practice Dostoyevsky's procedure is much different.

## NOTES

[1] Cf. a letter to Lyubimov, editor of *The Russian Messenger*, reprinted in *Dostoyevsky: A Self-Portrait* by Jessie Coulson (O.U.P. 1962), pp. 219–20.

[2] Edited and translated by Boris Brasol, in two volumes (Cassell, 1949).

[3] Coulson, op. cit., p. 220.

[4] See above, ch. I, particularly p. 10.

[5] 'Problems of Evil', *Sophia*, vol. i, 1965, p. 21. Referring initially to Ninian Smart's *Philosophers and Religious Truth*, S.C.M., 1964, Helm is indicating difficulties in any attempt to talk of *the* problem of evil solely as an epistemological problem.

[6] Op. cit., pp. 183–96.

[7] Cf. E. J. Simmons, *Introduction to Russian Realism*, ch. 3, p. 133.

[8] See above, ch. I, p. 21.

[9] *Tolstoy or Dostoyevsky* (Penguin, 1967), p. 308.

[10] *The Rebel*, Trans. Anthony Bower (Penguin, 1962), p. 51.

[11] In N. K. Smith, *The Credibility of Divine Existence*, ed. A. J. Porteous.

[12] Cf. in addition to the papers mentioned already by Cook Wilson and Malcolm, D. Z. Phillips 'Faith, Scepticism, and Religious Understanding' in *Faith and Philosophical Enquiry* (Routledge, 1970.)

# III

# Emotion, Atheism and Belief — I

... that the conception of God can only be realized by us with certain emotions ... is an essential characteristic of the conception.

The point has been reached at which we should further clarify the role of the emotions in Ivan's atheism. This will involve a philosophical digression, but its importance for our discussion is fundamental. The necessity of such a digression is made plain in the contrast which we have noticed between the nature of Ivan's atheism and the type of philosophical discussion of atheism and belief outlined in Chapter I. On the one hand there is the 'anglo-saxon' inclination towards the elimination of the consideration of emotion from the discussion of religious belief — the insistence upon 'dispassionate' consideration of the evidence for and against theistic belief. Now, in itself, dispassionate investigation is thoroughly commendable, provided that this practice is interpreted in a manner appropriate to the subject-matter under discussion. If, however, the subject-matter is the nature of religious belief, then it is *not* appropriate as 'dispassionate investigation' is often taken to imply, to omit from philosophical discussion altogether consideration of the role of emotion in religious belief.

This is pointed up by the second term in our contrast — the role of emotion in Ivan's atheism. My argument has been that an understanding of the nature of the atheism portrayed in Ivan Karamazov, is only possible if we turn our consideration towards the subtle fashion in which his affirmation 'I accept God' has detached that locution from the emotions of reverence, love and humility. Of course, in doing this he is only following in deliberate and reflective fashion the path which the Russian boys and their professors have already unwittingly prepared. But *his* conception of both atheism and belief is radically different from that of those whom he satirizes, for he realizes that the rejection of belief can focus upon the emotional content of belief in ways of which the Russian boys, and often it seems, English-speaking philosophers, are quite unaware. The discussion which follows can be seen in two mutually supporting ways: it is the elaboration of a lesson which through Ivan, Dostoyevsky has to teach contemporary philosophy, and it is also an appeal to contemporary philosophical techniques in the elucidation of Ivan's rejection of belief.

In Chapter I (p. 21) the following remark was quoted

That the conception of God can only be realized by us with certain emotions, is not only a very interesting fact but it is an essential characteristic of the conception.[1]

This claim by Cook Wilson is both striking and unclear. It does, however, insist that there is a very strong connection between emotion and religious belief, and as such provides an admirable starting point for the discussion of this topic.

The expression 'realized', related to both 'conceptions' and 'emotions' is a puzzling one and could suggest that our inquiry is basically one of empirical psychology. On that view we should be committed to a survey of the emotions aroused by or connected with certain thoughts. Apart from the general difficulties involved in setting up such an inquiry, it would be misguided, since what is at stake here, is not a question of what feelings are *caused* by which thoughts, but is rather one of the *conditions* to which one should appeal as satisfying the claim to have had certain thoughts. The implication of Cook Wilson's claim is that unless the thoughts in question are accompanied by certain emotions, then they do *not* count as 'realizing the conception of God'. The condition in question is necessary, if not sufficient.

Thoughts, however, are notoriously difficult entities to deal with, and for 'realizing a conception' as the focus of our inquiry I propose to substitute 'understanding an expression'. The inquiry can now proceed on two complementary fronts: (a) Is part, or the whole of what it means to use expressions, including the word 'God' correctly, to have certain feelings or emotions when one does so? (b) Is part, or the whole of what it means to understand someone using expressions including the word 'God' correctly, to be thus made aware that he is expressing certain emotions or feelings?

Perhaps the strongest sort of connection compatible with a positive answer to each of the foregoing questions would be the assertion of a semantic connection between sentences including the word 'God' . . . and the expression of emotion: that is to say, an account of the meaning of sentences including the word 'God' . . . might be given which parallels the account given of the meaning of ethical terms under one or other of the versions of the emotive theory of ethics.[2] On such a view sentences including the word 'God' would incorporate, as part or the whole of their meaning, the expression of certain emotions.

Now it is certainly true that sentences of this sort are often used to express emotion. This is true both colloquially, as for example,

May God have pity on you,

and in a ritual setting, as for example,

God is our refuge and our strength.

But it is not obvious that this is equally true of *all* uses of *all* such sentences. Clearly

God is our refuge and our strength

can be used in a variety of ways, assertively and non-assertively, which do not express emotions. Likewise there are many sentences including the word 'God' which are not used to express emotion, e.g.

When man submits God to moral judgement, he kills Him in his own heart.

This claim by Camus is a statement about the 'grammar' or logic of the word 'God' and it does not express emotions.

Let us now consider, however, whether perhaps those sentences which are asserted typically by a religious believer are such that in such typical uses the expression of emotion could constitute the *whole* of their meaning. This would indeed be a strong claim to make, but also an implausible one, as is easily seen from the following example:

If God has called me to be a medical missionary, then I shall go.

Minimally, however difficult it might be to establish the truth of the antecedent, a believer who asserted the above would reasonably be taken to be offering some sort of conditional commitment to a future course of action, and this would correctly be seen as *part* of the meaning of what he said. Similarly, to include only the expression of emotion in giving an account of the meaning of sentences including the word 'God', would be to omit much of what a believer takes himself to be doing, for a believer might be doing many different things in using such sentences, even within the Christian tradition alone. For example, he may be making recommendations, giving orders, asking questions, making historical claims, making predictions and so on.[3] It seems therefore that a more likely line of inquiry is the possibility that *part* of the meaning of sentences including the word 'God' can be accounted for in terms of the expression of emotion. At least in principle, this cuts across the division of such sentences (mentioned in Chapter I, particularly pp. 14–15) into the mutually exclusive groups of *either* those which are cognitive *or* those which are emotive, imperative, or in some other way expressive of attitudes.

There are, however, still problems facing even this weaker thesis about the connection between meaning and the expression of emotion. One such problem is that it has not been specified whether each use of such sentences expresses the *same* emotion, nor whether all such sentences express the same emotion. There are particular difficulties about the second of these options particularly in relation to the sorts of sentence including the word 'God' which might typically be uttered by an unbeliever, and to this we must return in due course. On the first option, it is again fairly clear that even such a sentence as,

May God have pity on you

could express rather different emotions, e.g. anger, or pity, or both simultaneously. This is indicative of a general problem about emotive theories, even in this weaker version: unless one weakens further the thesis, to restrict it to a very limited range of expressions connected only to particular emotions,[4] it may turn out that, as in the above example, it is not clear which emotion is being expressed. The corollary of this point is, of course, that the *way* in which one says something can contribute as much to the expression of emotion as the actual words used. As army privates, schoolboys the world over and P. G. Wodehouse's Jeeves are well aware, the word 'Sir' can be used to express emotions ranging from irritation through respect to condescending amusement.

A possible reply to this which retains as an option the suggestion that the expression of emotion is *part* of the meaning of sentences including the word 'God', or the word 'Sir', would be to argue that it is important to distinguish between primary and secondary uses of the terms in question. In the case of the use of 'Sir', the primary use of the term would be as a mark of respect, or as a recognition of authority. That the term can be used, as it was used by both Jeeves and the good soldier Schweik, in a secondary way is parasitic upon the primary use. The distinction drawn by means of the above example, however, is between two different uses of a term, both of which are expressive of emotions. I should, however, want to broaden the distinction between primary and secondary uses of terms to include not simply those uses of terms which are expressive of emotion, but to include the possibility of some expressions which have a primary use which includes the expression of emotion, and a secondary use which does not. Clearly the converse of this does hold for there are many expressions which are normally used in other ways, but which can be used in the expression of emotion: for example,

You have just cycled over my favourite azalea.

In this last instance, if the case were sufficiently important we could examine the whole complex of relationships and circumstances which make it clear that in saying this to his young nephew, Jones is expressing anger: but in this instance although the fact that it can be used in this way is connected to its descriptive meaning, we are not tempted to say that the expression of emotion constitutes even *part* of the meaning of the sentence in question. It may be possible, however, to construe sentences including the word 'God' not in this way, but rather as examples of sentences whose primary use may include the expression of emotion, but which may have secondary uses which do not.

There are many different cases to be distinguished here, but a broad division of secondary uses into three different categories will suffice for present purposes. My argument is that certain terms are such that some uses of sentences in which they are included, are correctly understood as partially expressive of emotions. The term 'God' is the one which is our present concern: the uses in question, of sentences such as 'I believe in God the Father Almighty', or 'In the beginning God created the Heaven and the Earth', I am calling 'primary uses'. There are at least three types of secondary use.

(i) In what some philosophers call 'non-assertive' uses of the sentences in question. These include some truth-functional compounds, e.g. 'If God created the Heaven and the Earth, then . . .', and also quotations (implicit or explicit) and *oratio obliqua*, e.g. the irreverent choir-boys who are running a sweepstake on the occurrence of a particular sentence in the vicar's sermon might give the half-way running as follows:

He has now said that God is not forgetful of even the smallest sacrifice, seven times.

This first sub-class of secondary uses is not here of further interest.

(ii) In situations where assertive use is made of such sentences, but where no emotion is expressed. This type subdivides into cases where the speaker is aware that there is a primary use, and cases where the speaker is unaware of this. The latter includes the Russian boys, the former could include non-believers discussing the content of religion with a believer, or rather differently, philosophers who redefine the concept of God in terms of a particular philosophical theory.

(iii) In situations where deliberate assertive use is made of such sentences to express emotions other than those which the believer would regard as appropriate. Ivan is a particularly striking case here, but many examples of blasphemy would suffice.

In the context of this chapter the third group of secondary uses is central. My argument is that such use of sentences is very different from the sort of witless sarcasm which takes the form of repeating one's opponent's words in elongated linguistic exaggerations. Such a fate can befall any use of any sentence unfortunate enough to displease sullen mediocrity. Sarcasm of this sort does not depend upon the emotive content of the utterance which it mimics: it is indiscriminate. The third group of secondary uses, however, is defined by the fact that it does depend upon the existence of primary, expressive uses. It is this fact which explains why Ivan's 'I accept God' would not be offensive to the Russian boys, for they have no primary use for this sentence, whereas it is offensive to Alyosha and, by implication, to Zossima.

These considerations constitute part of the grounds for classifying the uses in question as respectively 'primary' and 'secondary'. The other main grounds for this are to be found in the actual uses of these and similar assertions in the practice of religion. Appeal to 'the facts of ordinary language' has almost become a discredited form of philosophical argument, and that not without cause. But in this case, if in any at all, there is indisputable relevance in the points made by Kemp Smith[5] about the context in which the central affirmations of religion have their home.

In the light of this, we can begin to answer the two questions posed at the outset of the discussion. The first of these was (a) Is part or the whole of what it means to use some sentences including the word 'God' correctly, to express feelings or emotions when one does so? The possibility of this being the *whole* of the meaning of such expressions as they are typically used within the Christian religion has been ruled out. Also, it has been argued that in some (secondary) uses of such expressions, there is no such requirement for even *part* of the meaning residing in the expression of emotions.

What remains is the possibility that part of the meaning of the primary use of such sentences or utterances is to be found residing in the expression of emotion. One of the crucial questions which contemporary philosophy of religion poses for such a possibility is this[6]: (c) Is it essential that all secondary users of such utterances must, if they are to understand the utterances in question, also be primary users of the expressions in question? This is the form which the question of whether or not understanding presupposes belief, takes in the context of the present discussion. My own view is that a negative answer is the correct one here, but the grounds for this are complex and will require, in due course, a discussion of the relation between emotions and feelings. So far, we have the possibility of the position outlined at the beginning of this paragraph. Further elucidation of this can be derived from a consideration of our second question: (b) Is part of what it means to understand someone's primary use of expressions including the word 'God' correctly, to be thus made aware that he is expressing certain emotions or feelings?[7]

It is at this point that we must take account of the sort of comment drawn by Urmson, from Paul Ziff, about emotivist theories of ethics:

The emotivists . . . have . . . confused the task of stating the facts about the speech acts typical of ethical discourse with the task of giving an account of the meaning of such terms as 'good' and 'right'.[8]

Now, there is some force in such a remark, and its application to our present discussion would be as follows:

The present analysis confuses the task of stating the facts about speech acts typical of religious discourse with the task of giving an account of the meaning of sentences including the word 'God'.

The implication would be that although typically in their primary uses of these expressions religious believers do find the speech acts in question accompanied by certain emotions, this is not equivalent to claiming that the expression of emotions is part of the meaning of such utterances. This takes us back to the crucial point of whether the emotions which there undoubtedly are, are contingent accompaniments of some utterances of the sentences in question, or whether they are more closely related to the utterances than that.

Let us consider the case of an atheistic anthropologist attempting to understand what a group of Christian believers mean when they speak of God. One of the most central criteria of success would be whether or not he is able to successfully converse with the believers *about* their belief. There are many ways in which success can elude the anthropologist in such situations. One such way is that he might give offence to those to whom he speaks by the way in which he speaks. One of the easiest ways of giving offence is to disregard or to be ignorant of the emotions of one's fellow conversationalists. Thus to suggest to a man that his devotion to God was incompatible with his present state of poverty would not only be to misunderstand the motivations which can be part of religious belief, it may also be to give offence because it misjudges how shocking it would be to such a believer to suggest that poverty could be a reason for abandoning his belief in God. The point here is not that it is simply against the rules to be rich and to be a believer (although the New Testament gives us to understand that it is very difficult!), but that it would be offensive to suggest that economic success should begin to act as some sort of devotional barometer. The meaning of 'I believe in God', within at least certain forms of Christianity, *pace* Tawney, excludes the possibility of using personal economic success as the criterion of whether or not to believe. In the same way, in most colloquial uses of such expressions as 'I love my wife', or 'She is devoted to her husband' the meaning of what is said excludes the use of the economic viability of one's spouse as definitive of the relationship. To suggest otherwise is to give offence. Not to know this about the expressions 'I love my wife' or 'She is devoted to her husband' is to have less than a complete understanding of what these expressions mean. Likewise not to understand the many ways in which offence can be given when talking to a man about his belief in God is seriously to fail to grasp the full meaning of certain uses of sentences including the word 'God'. Thus to say to a believer 'Your belief in God is nothing more than a projection of certain psychological states arising from sexual and aggressive impulses of early childhood', is not only to say something which he would regard as incompatible with his beliefs, it is also to say something which he would regard as *prima facie* shocking and offensive. Similarly to tell him that he should not put his trust in a God who allows the stock-market index to fall so drastically is to misunderstand amongst other things the extent to which the affirmation 'I believe in God the Father Almighty, Maker of Heaven and Earth' is expressive of the emotions of reverence and awe. Both the misunderstanding in question, and the possibility of giving offence in that way, depend upon the expression of emotion being part of the meaning of the sentences in question as they occur in what I have been calling their 'primary' use.

Clearly the notion of a 'primary' use here is being made to bear a considerable weight and further delineation of its contours is required. The distinction between primary and secondary uses of an expression was introduced on page 45 above to allow for the possibility of certain utterances, whose original or typical use is to express one emotion, being used in fact to express rather different emotions. The distinction was broadened to include cases where there would seem to be a primary use of certain utterances to express emotions but a secondary use which was not expressive of emotions. Typical examples of the latter would include raising second order or meta-questions about the primary uses of such expressions. The distinction, however, is not the same as that between first-order and second-order discourse, for it would be part of the view under consideration that in a variety of ways a man may engage in first-order religious discourse while making non-primary use of sentences including the word 'God'. For example, anthropologists have to do this frequently in relation to the religious beliefs of communities whom they are studying. Unbelievers may do this in talking to believers. To make a mistake, however, is *not* to make secondary uses of such expressions *per se,* it is rather to make secondary uses of such expressions while unaware that there are primary uses which are expressive of certain emotions. Likewise the criteria that would indicate that a mistake has been made do not relate to whether or not the use of the utterance is in fact, expressing an emotion which the speaker has, but relate rather to the speaker's awareness of what will and will not give offence to the primary users of such expressions. A corollary of this is that for the speaker deliberately to give offence is not necessarily for him to make a mistake: it is the unintended offence which is the mark of ignorance.

The alternative and I hope clearer, account of the relation between belief in God and the emotions which I should like to set alongside that of Cook Wilson is as follows:

Part of the meaning of certain uses of sentences including the word 'God', resides in the fact that they express emotions. These uses I propose to call their 'primary' uses for two reasons (a) the sense of some other 'secondary' uses is parasitic upon these primary uses, and (b) one criterion of the correctness of many secondary uses of these sentences is the speaker's awareness of the part which the expression of emotion plays in their primary uses.

It is compatible with this view to assert both that one can understand the primary use of such sentences without ever using them in this primary way, and that one can make correct secondary uses of such sentences without ever making a primary use of them. Also, the ever-present possibility that an expression is only partially understood, whether in primary or secondary uses, cannot be ruled out.

Doubtless at this point some will feel the promptings of a general sceptical argument to which appeal is often made by believers who wish to protect their beliefs from critical discussion. How, it might be contended, can someone who has no primary use for sentences including the word 'God' possibly understand what those sentences mean in their primary use? The difficulty, it will be suggested, is particularly great for a view which insists that part of the meaning of such a use of the sentence is the expression of emotion: presumably a man who has no such primary use for the sentence in question is in this position because he does not have the emotion in question.

I do not think that this constitutes a serious objection to the position which I have outlined, but it will be instructive to examine the reasons for this. Initially there is a problem about the individuation and identification of emotions. One way of construing the above argument would be to substitute 'feeling' for 'emotion'. Then sentences including the word 'God' are regarded in their primary uses as being expressive of particular feelings. Apart from the general difficulties of any attempt to equate emotions with feelings which has been the subject of much comment in recent philosophy,[9] such an equation would have unpalatable consequences here. For example any sincere primary use of the sentence

I believe in God the Father Almighty, Maker of Heaven and Earth,

would include the expression of a particular feeling — say awe, or reverence. This would be an unacceptably stringent account. Consider the case of someone under extreme duress or torture being asked to recant such a belief. The above condition would rule out as a primary sincere use of the sentence in question its assertion by a man wracked with pain and weak from hunger, who in the face of his persecutors still whispers 'I believe. . .' despite his incapacity to have ( = be aware of) and thus to be truly expressing any of the feelings in question. Undoubtedly this is an extreme example, but such has been the fate of some who would in that moment, be regarded as having made classic affirmations of faith, i.e. classic primary uses of the sentence 'I believe in God the Father Almighty. . .'. This is not to exclude feelings from religious or any other emotions, but it is to refuse to equate feelings with emotion, and it would not be misleading to suggest that in addition to being a classic affirmation of faith the above example might also be regarded as a thorough-going expression of both reverence and awe.

This brings to attention the ways in which the concept of an emotion is wider than that of a feeling. One of the ways in which it is so, is to be seen in the rich explanatory power which emotion-concepts have in the interpretation of tracts of behaviour.[10] This is not to assume, however, that the explanations in question are necessarily causal explanations. The purpose of an explanation is to help make some thing or event intelligible. In this sense to see someone's behaviour as expressive of certain emotions is to find an explanation for his deeds or words. Thus the utterance of the persecuted believer can be interpreted along with his perseverance as expressive of the emotion of reverence or awe for his God, quite independently of any feelings which he may at that moment be experiencing. This is not a peculiarity of religious emotions, as we can see in the case of grief: a man's quietness in company, and his preference for less boisterous pastimes than usual can be expressive of grief without assuming that he is throughout that quietness, or even as he refuses an invitation to the office party, subject to specific feelings.

An alternative way of construing the general sceptical argument would be to argue, not that for 'emotion' we should read 'feeling', but that even granted a broader conception of emotion, those who have not had the emotions in question cannot understand the sentences, and this is why they have no primary use for them. One way in which the argument gains *prima facie* plausibility is that it depends upon the unstated premiss that the meaning of emotion words, or words expressive of emotions, is both established and learned by correlating the words in question with private experiences. Now the philosophical discussion of this and related points is considerable and it would be out of place here to survey the whole literature.[11] None the less three general difficulties can be raised: first, it is difficult to see how on this view we come to have what we evidently do have, that is, a public and shared language including terms of the sort under discussion; second, it is also difficult to see, as Wittgenstein pointed out in the *Philosophical Investigations*[12] how the person who has the private experience in question could *re-identify* a later occurrence of that experience as the same as the one he had previously; third, one highly contentious aspect of the assumption in question is the view that the feelings are contingently related to the complex of behaviour beliefs and deeds which surround them.

Even apart from these general problems, however, there are other issues here which relate more directly to the specifically religious context of the discussion. I have already granted that the broader account of emotions does not exclude feelings from being part, in some cases a constituent part, of what emotions are. I should want to insist, however, upon a distinction between emotions and feelings at least in so far as it is true that one's behaviour can express an emotion without it following that one has, during that period, any specific feelings, e.g. behaviour expressive of grief but not entailing that one feels sad at that particular moment. To make the point more precise, for the correct attribution of those emotions which we might regard as religious, on most but not all occasions feelings are a necessary but not a sufficient condition. One implication of this is that I am not countering the present objection by trying to produce a wholly dispositional analysis of the religious emotions, nor do I think that such an enterprise would be successful. This leaves open two questions: (a) In those cases where correct attribution of religious emotions does include the condition that a person has specific feelings, what other conditions must be satisfied?; and (b) Which features of the emotions in question lead us to talk of them as *religious* emotions?

A complete answer to (a) is not necessary for present purposes, nor in view of the discussion which it would require is it appropriate. Suffice it to point out that the other conditions are largely of a public or observable nature and they would include reference to a man's previous and subsequent behaviour, a capacity to predict how in certain situations he would decide and act, in some cases a description of the social context within which we are led to make the attribution, a man's moral commitments as revealed in his actions and dispositions to action, what he says about himself in the situation in question and so on. The crucial point about an answer to (b) is whether what makes an emotion religious is something distinctive about the *feelings* which are part of the emotion, or whether it is to be found in other aspects of the situation. There has been much confused disagreement arising out of the failure to distinguish between these two possibilities in the history of the Christian Church.

Now there is a readiness on the part of many to assume that what is distinctive about religious emotions is that they are partly constituted by unusual or idiosyncratic feelings whose difference from other feelings is what makes them religious. However, if one looks closely at even those different episodes in the history of Christianity which might be thought to lay greatest emphasis upon the 'private' or 'inner' feelings as what is distinctively religious, the support for this analysis of the religious emotions appears much less substantial than one might assume. For example St. Teresa found to her cost that what she happened to *feel* in her meditative life was the most unreliable of guides to her spiritual progress, and that the drive to arouse within oneself certain specifically religious feelings would prove to be destructive of the practice of religious meditation.[13] In a very different context Jonathan Edwards, appalled by the consequences of allowing to feeling a definitive role in the assessment of the religious emotions aroused in the New England religious revivals of his time wrote *The Nature of the Religious Affections*[14] in which he followed the Johannine Epistles of the New Testament in subjugating feeling to behaviour and disposition in his account of the nature of the religious emotions. A third supporting example here is St. Paul. From what we read in the various New Testament accounts of his conversion experience, what distinguished his emotions and their religious quality from those of his fellow travellers on the road to Damascus seems to have had everything to do with the role which these emotions play in interpreting his subsequent behaviour and nothing to do with his inner feelings at the time.[15]

Now none of this is to deny that feelings are important to religion, let alone to the religious emotions. What I do want to offer is an account of the religious emotions which makes what is religiously distinctive about these emotions, those elements of the emotions other than particular feelings. If this account is the correct one, and the most I must establish here is the negative side of it, then even on the wider view of the nature of the emotions there seems to be no adequate ground for insisting that someone who has no primary use for sentences including the word 'God' (i.e. no emotively expressive use) cannot understand what is the meaning of the sentences so used. If what makes the emotions so expressed distinctively religious is *not* the only likely candidate for the sort of privacy which might debar the secondary user from a thorough grasp of what is being expressed, then there seem no obvious impediments to understanding.

The plausibility of the position which I am adopting here gains strength in so far as the following possible scenario of the situation in question can be fairly easily imagined. We are now in a position to argue that the feelings which are a part of the religious awe or reverence expressed in some primary uses of sentences including the word 'God', are not distinctively religious feelings, i.e. are not peculiar to the religious emotions. As such, even allowing for the sake of argument, that in as strong a sense as is desired these feelings are private and are correlated with terms which name them by an act of introspection, this provides no inevitable bar to the understanding of what we are calling secondary-users. If these feelings are not distinctively religious then there is no reason why secondary-users might not have had the feelings in question in contexts which are not overtly, or even covertly religious, e.g. in the contemplation of works of creative genius, in the discovery of the depth of love between two people, in the presence of a man whose integrity is impressive, or for someone such as Kant on the contemplation of 'the moral law within and the starry heavens above'.

Two concluding comments before proceeding to summarize and move to the next stage in the argument: on this account what makes a religious emotion religious will be discovered either in one or some of those elements of the emotion which are not private in the strong sense allowed, or in the complex structure of those elements and any relevant feelings which together are sufficient conditions for the correct attribution of religious awe or reverence;[16] although 'for the sake of argument' I have posited an account of the relation between feelings and language which sees the former as private and the latter as providing names for these private feelings, this is not an account which other than 'for the sake of argument' I should be prepared to accept, but the reasons for that, hinted at above, are not central to the present discussion.

What I have been trying to do so far in this chapter is to present a reasonably clear and defensible account of a connection between religious belief and the emotions recognized to some extent by Cook Wilson, and summarized above as follows:

Part of the meaning of certain uses of sentences including the word 'God' resides in the fact that they express emotions. These uses I propose to call their primary uses for two reasons (a) the sense of other 'secondary' uses is parasitic upon these primary uses, and (b) one criterion of the correctness of many secondary uses of these sentences is the speaker's awareness of the part which the expression of emotion plays in their primary uses.

Our discussion must now move to a different plane — to a discussion of the significance of all this for clarifying the role of the emotions in Ivan's atheism. If the implications of the above analysis of the primary uses of certain sentences including the word 'God' are accepted, then we can begin to see more clearly how it is possible that atheism, the rejection of belief in God, can take a variety of different forms. If part of the meaning of certain affirmations of belief in God, is to express certain religious emotions, then the attempt to make use of these affirmations in a way that is not expressive of emotion, or the attempt to use them to express radically different emotions could constitute the rejection of belief. In Ivan we find both of these forms of atheism.

His 'I accept God' can be taken in a number of different ways, each of which, as I have already argued in the previous chapter, is in fact a rejection of belief in God. At one level his acceptance of God is the acceptance of the God of the Russian boys. The acceptance of God is then one in which the emotions play no part. The affirmation 'I accept God', as used by Ivan, mimics the affirmations of 'faith' which he sees open to the Russian boys and their Professors: it is not expressive of emotion, either in the narrow sense of feelings, nor in the broader sense of providing explanatory hypotheses for tracts of their behaviour. The idea of feeling religious awe or reverence, 'while snatching a free moment in a pub', is comic: nor can we explain their participation in the speculative blether about God and his purposes in terms of a sense of worship. To use the utterance 'I accept God' in *this* way is to misuse it: to misuse it thus *deliberately* is to reject belief in God. In a comparable way, the man who says to his terrified friend 'Very well, you did see a ghost, but now let's get to sleep again', rejects his friend's belief quite as firmly as if he had argued convincingly that the evidence for the existence of ghosts is very thin indeed. (The difference between this case and Ivan's atheism, however, is that I have argued that in its primary use part of the meaning of an utterance such as 'I believe in God' or 'I accept God', is the expression of the emotion of awe and reverence: it is more debatable whether part of the *meaning* of 'There is a ghost in this house' is the expression of fear, although in some uses, the sentence can certainly serve precisely this function.)

At a different level Ivan's acceptance of God is his expression of a very powerful emotion: that of moral outrage. Of the suffering of children, he protests

Why should they too be used as dung for someone's future harmony?

The outrage is partly focused upon those who would attempt to give an answer to that question — the proponents of some form of theodicy. Partly, however, it is focused upon the figure of God, and that is what leads to Alyosha's insistence that 'This is rebellion'. Ivan's emotions are both complex and volatile, and he is himself often unaware of their strength and profundity. Occasionally these volcanic depths erupt, though more characteristically they seep to the surface of his relationships with others and congeal in an apparent detachment. One such eruption is over the cruelty of men to children, and even from Alyosha he wrings the venomous 'Shoot him' as the sentence which befits the crime of a man who sets his hounds to hunt down a small child. To accept a God who has incorporated such a scene in a drama which moves towards final harmony is to express a variety of emotions — venom, bitterness and despair. When Dostoyevsky insists

Even in Europe there have never been atheistic expressions of such power[17]

he is appealing to the protest of Ivan which in the apparent affirmation of faith substitutes for the emotions of awe and reverence those of bitterness and anger. To do this intentionally, as Ivan does, is to play upon the expressive content of traditional confessions of faith as a means of producing a rejection of faith elusive in its subtlety, yet piercing in its accuracy. It is thus to produce a form of atheism whose distinctive feature consists neither of a negation of the statement

'God exists', nor of a compilation of evidence to suggest that God does not exist. It has, however, to do with the meaning of utterances which include the word 'God' but not in the way that Ayer's form of atheism focuses upon criteria of meaning.

## NOTES

[1] J. Cook Wilson, op. cit.

[2] See C. L. Stevenson, 'The Emotive Meaning of Ethical Terms' (*Mind*, 1937) and *Ethics and Language* (Yale U.P., 1944). For a more recent account of issues raised by Stevenson and others, see J. O. Urmson, *The Emotive Theory of Ethics* (O.U.P., 1968).

[3] A similar series of points was made in response to Braithwaite's simplistic analysis of the meaning of religious assertions. See, for example, the reprint of Braithwaite's *An Empiricist's View of the Nature of Religious Belief* in I. T. Ramsey (ed.), *Christian Ethics and Contemporary Philosophy* (S.C.M., 1966), and the papers in comment upon it by Schofield, MacKinnon and Ramsey.

[4] Such expressions could include for example direct first person claims about the speaker's emotional states, e.g. 'I fear an attack', or *possibly* expletives or expressions of irritation like 'She's late again, damn her'.

[5] See the quotation from Kemp Smith in Chapter II above, pp. 35–6.

[6] See for example J. Hick (ed.), *Faith and the Philosophers*, pp. 115–55, which consisted of a paper by A. MacIntyre, and comments by Norris Clarke, Richard Brandt, and William Alston.

[7] This is a version of (b) amended to take account of points already made.

[8] J. O. Urmson, op. cit., p. 136.

[9] See particularly A. Kenny, *Action, Emotion and Will* (Routledge & Kegan Paul, 1963).

[10] See A. Kenney, op. cit., and E. Bedford, 'Emotions', in *The Philosophy of Mind*, ed. V. C. Chappell (Prentice-Hall, 1962).

[11] See for example the papers collected in O. R. Jones (ed.), *The Private Language Argument* (Macmillan, 1967).

[12] L. Wittgenstein, *Philosophical Investigations* (Blackwell, 1953).

[13] See E. W. Trueman Dicken, *The Crucible of Love* (Darton, Longman & Todd, 1963).

¹⁴ Yale U.P. 1959.

¹⁵ Confirmation of this can be found in examination of the various accounts of this event, both retold in the third person, and also as attributed to St. Paul himself, in the Book of Acts. See particularly Acts 9: 1–9, 22: 1–11, and 26: 1–21. The historical accuracy of the Book of Acts is neither here nor there for present purposes, for our interest is in the Pauline experience which has become for many Christians definitive of genuine religious experience: and *that* experience is the one to be found in the Book of Acts.

¹⁶ See G. E. Moore, *Principia Ethica*, pp. 27 ff. His account of the principle of organic unity makes a suggestion in the field of ethics which has analogies to the second of the options outlined here.

¹⁷ See E. J. Simmons, *Introduction to Russian Realism*, ch. 3, p. 133.

# IV

## Emotion, Atheism and Belief—II

*If it can't be decided in the affirmative, it will never be decided in the negative. You know that that is the peculiarity of your heart. . .*

There are a number of points raised in or suggested by the last chapter which require further discussion. The general direction of the argument in this chapter will be the converse of that followed in the previous chapter: whereas, there, an examination of some general philosophical issues led to a more detailed discussion of Ivan Karamazov, in what follows our point of departure will be Ivan, and the more general philosophical issues will be allowed to arise out of the problems posed for us by this fictitious character.

One of the more obvious ways in which superficial judgement can lead us to misinterpret the figure of Ivan is in over-emphasizing Ivan's intellectual qualities. Reason and rationality were important to Ivan, and in the Karamazov family Ivan was distinguished from the others by his intellectual gifts. He had returned to the family home with a reputation which was based upon these gifts and the place which they had won for him in the sophisticated and cultured society of Moscow. Whatever interpretations are made of his famous article on punishment in the context of the Church and the State, it was assuredly the work of a most ingenious mind. He had also the outward marks which many take to be typical of the intellectual— a certain aloofness and detachment combined with a rather cynical but quick turn of mind. It is easy to remain preoccupied with Ivan's 'ideas' and to discuss him wholly in terms of his intellect. Ronald Hingely, for example, confines his discussion of Ivan very largely to the picture of Ivan, who as representing 'the Mind' in the allegorical linking of the three legitimate brothers to Body, Mind and Soul respectively, is portrayed as 'the intellectual heretic' who acquires in the novel a series of 'ideological satellites'.[1]

Undoubtedly Ivan is an intellectual, and doubtless his allegorical position in the novel can be seen as Hingely suggests, but as Hingely also admits the three brothers are more than allegorical units, they are individuals. Apart from all else, an acquaintance with Dostoyevsky's other major novels would teach us to expect no less of Ivan than we find in Dostoyevsky's other intellectual heroes. Raskolnikov, Stavrogin, Kirilov, each of these in his own way a man of intellect, finds his life governed by subterranean rivers of passion: and in Raskolnikov, as in the narrator of *Letters from the Underworld* we find Dostoyevsky's biting comment upon the hopes of Chernyshevsky and his followers for a utopian society whose members were solely moved to action by rational principles, albeit those of rational self-interest. Ivan belongs to this same stream of thought: man cannot and does not live by the intellect alone.

In the novel many pointers turn our attention to the emotions and their role in Ivan's life. Part of the difficulty in understanding him is not that he lacks emotion, but that his emotions are in turmoil: in their spasmodic impact on his behaviour they do not provide a clear guide to his character. The imagery of his comment on the brawling of Dmitri and old Karamazov suggests the serpent-like venom of his aggressive impulses:

One reptile will devour the other. And serve them both right too.[2]

On the other hand, like his brother Dmitri he too can quote Schiller, 'which Alyosha would never have believed'.[3] He displays excitement and passion, both in his narration of the Legend of the Grand Inquisitor, and in his outburst of moral outrage at the cruelty of men to children. He does share with his brothers the legacy of the Karamazov baseness and tells Alyosha that this will provide him with the strength to endure in his chosen plan 'to live on to thirty, and then . . . dash the cup to the ground': and yet one always senses that his love of life, of 'the sticky little leaves', is a profound driving force. At times he is conscious of his own capacity for emotion and admits that if he did make his pilgrimage to the shrines of Europe,

I know beforehand that I shall fall down on the ground and kiss the stones and weep over them . . . I shall get drunk on my own emotion.

Over against this, however, he often withdraws from his emotions, pushing them aside as he does his poem of the Grand Inquisitor:

Why, it's all nonsense Alyosha. It's only a senseless poem of a senseless student, who could never write two lines of verse. Why do you take it so seriously?

Or occasionally he puts between himself and the conscious engagement of the emotions the irony of an elaborate but not wholly trivial joke — as in his article, about which he tells Zossima, 'But I wasn't altogether joking.'

What then, are we to make of Ivan and his emotions and what is their significance for his atheism? In the previous chapter we discovered how he used the language of religious confession in such a way as to distort its emotive content either by removing that emotive content in mimicking the bar-room discussion of 'the eternal questions', or by using the utterances in question to express emotions other than those of love, awe, and reverence. The rather different question now being raised is whether the emotions which we may attribute to Ivan, play a different, but comparably non-accidental role in the structure of his atheism. We are certainly made aware of the tensions within Ivan's psyche, perhaps most acutely in his dialogue with the devil whom he creates to mock himself. How do these internal divisions relate to his rejection of belief? Dostoyevsky's knowledge of human nature is too great to allow a cheap and superficial equation of disintegration and the refusal of belief. What alternatives remain?

One view of Ivan which many critics adopt is to see in him a battle in Pascalian terms, between the head and the heart, and then to apply to Ivan his own comment on the Grand Inquisitor whom Christ silently kisses on the cheek and then leaves:

The kiss glows in his heart, but the old man adheres to his idea.

This is the Ivan to whom Richard Peace points:

Thus there is in Ivan an emotional side to his nature which his intellect is scarcely able to understand: his dilemma is that of 'loving life rather than the meaning of life,' whilst his intellect demands meaning.[4]

The intellect and the emotions have been philosophically at war from Plato to Kant and beyond, and it is tempting to rest content with this view of Ivan. There is, however, another side to the story which we should not overlook. Ivan is undecided and indecisive in his thinking and in some of his attitudes, and particularly in his ambivalence towards the emotions which he feels.

Examples of this last ambivalence have already been noted above. Zossima pinpoints both this and Ivan's indecision on the question of immortality in a diagnosis of Ivan's state of mind and emotion to which Ivan gives symbolic assent in his acceptance of the Elder's blessing:

'You were not altogether joking. That's true. The question is still fretting your heart, and not answered. But the martyr likes sometimes to divert himself with his despair, as it were driven to it by despair itself. Meanwhile, in your despair, you, too divert yourself with magazine articles, and discussions in society, though you don't believe your own arguments, and with an aching heart mock at them inwardly . . . that question you have not answered, and it is your great grief, for it clamours for an answer.'

The indecisiveness here, if Zossima is correct, is in part about belief: 'Can that question be answered by me?' Ivan asks. It is, however, partly of, and about, the emotions: Ivan might ask of himself, as we ask of him, whether or not he really does despair and grieve. Is he not rather ironically and cynically amused at those who worry over such questions? Does he really grieve over his despair, or does he not rather scorn such despair? In part, this is for Ivan a question of self-knowledge and as such it takes two forms: (a) What *does* he actually feel? What are his emotions?; and (b) What *ought* he to feel?—What *value* does he place on the reluctance to jettison concern with these issues completely—a reluctance which Zossima characterizes as follows:

If it can't be decided in the affirmative, it will never be decided in the negative. You know that that is the peculiarity of your heart, and all its suffering is due to it.

Ivan is both divided within himself and unsure of himself. His enigmatic exterior screens from himself, as well as from others, a complex inner turmoil.

He surprises himself just as he surprises those around him, be it in the way in which after years of silence he 'reels off a rigmarole like that' to Alyosha in the pub. And as his contemporaries are puzzled about his article on state and ecclesiastical courts, so those with him are amazed at the way in which he moves to accept Zossima's blessing. Again, does he speak with compassion when he cries out over the cruelties which children endure? Or is it as Mochulsky suggests 'on his lips . . . pure rhetoric'?[5] If it is compassion, what has happened to that compassion as he knocks over a drunk peasant and passing on his way simply notes 'He will be frozen'? And how is this callousness to be reconciled with his reaction as he reappears from Smerdyakov's cottage, and becomes the good samaritan to this half-covered body in the snow whom he had left to freeze an hour before?

The irregular and unpredictable pattern of his actions can clearly be explained in terms of irregularity of the emotions. What significance, however, can we attach to the irregularity of his emotions? Does this have anything to tell us of the nature of his atheism? The thesis of this chapter is that it does, and in discovering just why this is so we shall learn something about Ivan, about atheism, and about a further series of connections between the emotions and religious belief.

It was suggested in the previous chapter that one of the ways in which the role of the emotions in religious belief reveals itself, is in the emotive content of primary uses of certain utterances including the word 'God'. There is a rather different but quite compatible way in which the importance of the emotions for any account of religious belief emerges. Put in general terms it is this: the difference between some forms of belief and some forms of atheism has to do with the connections which hold between these two possibilities and respectively *different* emotions.

One way of trying to be more specific would be to argue that as a matter of contingent fact we find that people react in different ways, with different emotions to what otherwise seems to be the same situation. Thus Dostoyevsky's reaction to the Holbein painting 'The Deposition' in Switzerland was undoubtedly very different from that of many other visitors. In another context the maudlin sentiment which accompanies old Karamazov's assertions of belief, are very different on the one hand from Ivan's outrage and rebellion, and on the other hand from the emotions which were evoked in Zossima as he turned, in his early manhood, from indifference to belief. Not only could we suggest that these emotions are *as a matter of fact* different from one man to another, we could even offer an explanation of why this is so, of the sort that Rakitin derives from Claude Bernard and offers to Dmitri. Dmitri, in turn, stumblingly explains to Alyosha:

Imagine: inside, in the nerves, in the head— that is, these nerves are there in the brain . . . (damn them!) there are sort of little tails, the little tails of those nerves, as soon as they begin quivering, those little tails . . . and when they quiver an image appears . . . it doesn't appear at once, but an instant, a second passes . . . and then something like a moment appears; that is, not a moment— devil take the moment!— but an image; that is, an object, or an action, damn it! That's why I see and then think, because of those tails, not at all because I've got a soul, and that I am some sort of image and likeness. All that is nonsense! Rakitin explained it all to me yesterday, brother, and it simply bowled me over.

Now clearly the use of drugs to alleviate the depressive or euphoric symptoms of mental illness lends weight to such a view as this. Notwithstanding, I want to reject the over-simple view of the relationship of the emotions to religious belief and atheism which simply claims that 'It's chemistry.' That does less than justice to the complex ways in which emotions belong to the texture of our beliefs and attitudes, particularly within the context of religion.

On Rakitin's view the role which the emotions play in Ivan's, or indeed Alyosha's life, would be best understood in terms of the chemistry of their respective bodies. An alternative view is to regard the emotions as constituent parts of larger belief-systems, or patterns of life. Ivan does experience a variety of emotions, and it is reasonable to ask what relations hold between these emotions and his atheism. My argument will be at first a general one that some forms of atheism are what they are because of the emotions which they embody. We shall then turn to the more particular question of the significance of this in Ivan's case.

When Ivan insisted to Alyosha that he cannot accept God's world and that 'I most respectfully return Him the ticket,' Alyosha murmurs 'That's rebellion.'

'Rebellion? I am sorry you call it that,'said Ivan earnestly. 'One can hardly live in rebellion, and I want to live' (p. 252).

If the picture of Ivan's emotions does contain a unity (and whether it does is debatable), then the unity is that of rebellion: his emotions as they appear, are those of concern, anger and moral outrage. They are accompanied by an ironical streak which serves to mask the possibility of hatred and pride, both of which have been attributed to Ivan by a number of commentators. His rebellion, his refusal to accept the world, is at the heart of his atheism, and already we have seen the way in which he uses his rebellion as a means of limiting the role which the concept of God can play to the trivial and the insignificant.

What must now be discussed is the range of the emotions which belong to rebellion.

It is not disputed that anger, and some form of moral outrage belong there. What, however, of compassion, of concern for others? Is this rebellion genuinely concerned with the needs of others? Is it, in that sense, *moral* rebellion? Atheism and religious belief often engage in dispute over the middle-ground of morality, and the question of whether or not a life based on rebellion, or revolt, is a genuine expression of moral concern, is one of the less unprofitable areas of discussion. The intention in what follows is the analysis rather than the resolution of the dispute. The hope is that this will tell us something of the nature of Ivan's atheism.

Camus's question about rebellion is the appropriate one here: Can *limits* be set to rebellion? The answers of religious writers such as Simone Weil and Soren Kierkegaard agree in denying that there are such limits. In *The Rebel*, Camus argued that it is possible to set moral limits to rebellion, and that it does make sense to talk of rebellion as an act of compassion, and to see it as expressive of human love and concern for others. He is, of course, dealing here not with the comparatively easy case of a particular protest about a particular moral or political outrage, but with the much more difficult and elusive question of whether, in Alyosha's words one can 'live by' rebellion, and do so in a manner that is compatible with the moral ideals of love and care for one's fellow human beings. Ivan's indecisiveness as he comes increasingly to see it himself, includes precisely this question. The ambiguity over his attitude to the needs of others is Dostoyevsky's way of raising this question in the reader's mind. What are the parallels in the novel for Ivan's concern for others? Are they to be found in Zossima and Alyosha, or should we compare Ivan's 'compassion' to that of the God whose theodicy he rejects, or of his brother Dmitri's treatment of Katya and Snegiryov? The answer to these questions betray much about the kind of atheism being offered for our consideration.

Camus characterizes one of the central religious responses to rebellion with both lucidity and economy:

When man submits God to moral judgment, he kills him in his own heart.

Certainly one of the reasons for rejection of rebellion by many Christians has been the incompatibility of moral condemnation and attitudes of reverence and care. Ivan exemplifies the logic of this, as it has been traced out in the previous two chapters. Kierkegaard sets a different question mark against rebellion which has more to do initially with the self-image and self-identity of the rebel than it has to do with his image of God. In *Sickness Unto Death*, he writes:

Revolting against the whole of existence, it (demoniac despair) thinks it has hold of a proof against it, against its goodness. This proof the despairer thinks he himself is, and that is what he wills to be, therefore he wills to be himself, himself with his torment, in order with this torment to protest against the whole of existence. Whereas the weak despairer will not hear about what comfort eternity has for him, so neither will such a despairer hear about it, but for a different reason, namely, because this comfort would be the destruction of him as an objection against the whole of existence. (pp. 118–19, O.U.P.)

The relation of revolt to despair is not our present concern, and at this stage of our discussion could only be viewed as a psychological relation, in which, interestingly Kierkegaard is suggesting that despair is the causal factor and revolt the effect. The primary interest in the above quotation lies in the suggestion that revolt or rebellion against existence is a means of giving oneself an identity. If this is the case, then clearly a belief in the goodness of God would threaten that identity and vice-versa.

Is rebellion then, inevitably a means of giving oneself an identity, or a means of creating a self-image? Clearly it *can* be this, and the romantic excesses of such a view are Kierkegaard's primary targets in his discussion of 'strong despair' in *Sickness Unto Death*. Camus was also critical of rebellion which is romantic posture, but he seems to endorse the view *and* vindicate the value of a rebellion which is initially an act of *self*-assertion. In *The Rebel* he talks of rebellion as in the first instance '*my own* protest' (my italics). Implicit in his analysis, however, is a realization that such self-assertion, if guided only by historical expediency, becomes another form of tyranny. This is why at the end of *The Rebel*, he wants to insist that rebellion must be distinguished from resentment, and that it can be, but only in so far as one insists that 'rebellion cannot exist without a strange form of love'. Camus is an atheist who believes that rebellion is compatible with 'a strange form of love'. Kierkegaard implies that it is not. Simone Weil has a view which suggests that Camus's hope of a combination of anger, moral outrage, compassion and love is a vain one: self-assertion cannot grow progressively into love that is self-less.

Her fear was that in becoming rebellion — 'the revolt against existence'— what began as an act of compassion for others becomes an act of self-assertion. As such it would have left compassion behind. The significance of this argument, however, is not simply that of a belief about the contingent facts of human psychology: it has to do with what she saw as the conceptual connections between acceptance and compassion. What Simone Weil means by the 'acceptance' of affliction and suffering, whether in one's own case or in the case of others, is nothing more nor less than 'attention'. Attention which is complete and absolute is the form of love, whether the love of God or the love of one's neighbour. Attention as such is a form of self-emptying: it is the contemplation of and absorption into what is other than oneself. As such, Simone Weil believed attention and therefore love and compassion, to be incompatible with rebellion:

Those who rebel in the presence of affliction would like to be something.

To want to be something is in the end the basic form of self-assertion. When self comes into the picture, one has to that extent diverted or averted one's eyes: one no longer attends to the affliction. This, I take it, is what Simone Weil means when she argues that rebellion consists in averting one's eyes, and that 'acceptance is nothing else than the quality of attention'.

The above brief digression into Simone Weil's writings is offered as an elaboration, comparable to the one offered by Camus of the implications of Ivan's rebellion. The divergence between belief and atheism which the figure of Ivan illuminates is a disagreement about the value of certain emotions — anger and moral outrage — as they are directed towards the world or its alleged creator. Camus sees the anger and outrage of rebellion as of potentially fundamental value in coming to terms with the world in which we live, while at the same time, in Ivan's words 'sticking to the facts'. Simone Weil sees this form of anger and outrage as ultimately destructive of love and compassion. If it is and remains rebellion, she believes, then it is a form of self-assertion which distracts our attention from the needs of others. It must be emphasized here that she, along with Camus and Dostoyevsky, is concerned with rebellion as a primary and pervasive form of response to the world in which we live.

There is a rather different form of non-acceptance, of rebellion, which she does find acceptable:

[If, . . . he (Ivan Karamazov) were to say: 'I won't accept— not a single tear shall be shed over and above what is strictly outside my power to prevent'— he would possess the implicit love of God.]

But, of course, Ivan does *not* say this. [Nor, incidentally, does he spend much time preventing the tears of children: in that respect he does seem to be rather like the God whom he indicts.] His rebellion, his non-acceptance is, in that sense, a matter of *theoria* rather than *praxis*; and the point here is that it is a manner of primary response to the whole of what Christians call 'creation', not a selective response which is the motive to the prevention of suffering.

In summary this chapter has taken the form of an argument that the ambiguous pattern of Ivan's emotions is significant as a further means of understanding his atheism. The ambiguity which shows itself in the uncertain role of Ivan's various emotions is not itself a constitutive part of his atheism: but in so far as it is an uncertainty about the value to be placed on his various emotions, and about their compatibility one with another, then this irresolution points to a dispute about the nature of the anger and outrage of rebellion. This dispute is very much a product of the nineteenth century and was central to the dialogue which Camus carried on in his notebook and writings with the thoughts of Simone Weil. The general view which this analysis supports is that the difference between certain forms of atheism and certain forms of belief resides in a disagreement about the value and significance of certain sorts of emotions and feelings. The particular conclusion is that Ivan's struggle with his emotions, lying beneath the surface of his humour, was the struggle of one who was torn between the emotions of rebellion and the unacceptability of the apparent consequences, that compassion and concern for others are incompatible with rebellion. In posing Ivan's dilemma in this way Dostoyevsky seems to be in agreement with Kierkegaard and Simone Weil rather than Camus, but there is more of the novelist's instinct for the ambiguities of human existence in this, than there is an attempt to resolve the issue at stake. Intellectually the words of Ivan present the case for atheism: in literary terms, the blurring of the edges of Ivan's character, the enigmatic exterior's relation to the turbulent interior of his life, show us something of the nature of the divergence between atheism and belief. This is part of the fascination which Ivan has for the twentieth century. It is not simply, as some critics seem to suggest; that Ivan's cynicism and unbelief make him more interesting than the innocent and believing Alyosha.

## NOTES

[1] Ronald Hingely, *The Undiscovered Dostoyevsky* (Hamish Hamilton, 1962). See particularly chapter 10.

[2] Constance Garnett, Heinemann trans. p. 142.

[3] Ibid., p. 196.

[4] Richard Peace, *Dostoyevsky* (Cambridge University Press, 1971), p. 235.

[5] K. Mochulsky, op. cit., p. 616.

# V

# Ivan and the Grand Inquisitor

Christ-like love for men is a miracle impossible on earth.

A study of *The Brothers Karamazov* which omitted discussion of the Legend of the Grand Inquisitor would be the paradigm of a literary miscarriage. Yet this strange and haunting tale already in its simplicity and elegance indicts the sheer volume of writing devoted to its exegesis. Necessity, however, takes precedence over reluctance and this chapter will add further to what has already been written on the subject.

Few would disagree with Berdyaev's judgement:

The Legend of the Grand Inquisitor is the high point of Dostoyevsky's work and the crown of his dialectic,[1]

but beyond that there seem to be as many interpretations as there are readers. Dostoyevsky himself regarded the legend as crucially important and referred to it as 'the culminating point' of the whole novel. Agreement as to importance, however, does not guarantee agreement as to what it is in the story that is important. At times Dostoyevsky seems to hold up to the reader a mirror in which one sees reflected one's own values and tacit metaphysical beliefs.

Perhaps the most striking divergence in the various readings of the tale is exemplified by two Christian writers. Romano Guardini argues that the legend offers to us a Christ who is in the end a heretic, a Christ who 'is not truly the Word',[2] whereas Berdyaev argues that Dostoyevsky here offers us an 'extremely powerful vindication of Christ'.[3] Some have seen in the legend a reactionary political attack on all forms of socialism, whereas others have stressed the extent to which the range of Dostoyevsky's critique includes within its compass not only totalitarian regimes, but also, those refusals of freedom which are concealed, beneath the language and outward forms of the industrial democracies.[4]

This remarkable unity of mind on the quality of this 'unique essay in the philosophy of history . . . nearly without equal in world literature',[5] combined with complete interpretative disarray,[6] is a strange but powerful witness to Dostoyevsky's genius. It leaves further commentators with an unenviable task, which in this essay will be rendered slightly less intolerable by restricting comment to those aspects of the story which will add to our picture of Ivan's atheism.

Initially we ought to remind ourselves of the setting of the tale. It is Ivan's prose poem which he recounts to Alyosha, as they 'get acquainted'. Ivan has rejected the possibility of an adequate theodicy, and along with that, any acceptable way of talking about God. Alyosha's response, without quite conceding that there is no satisfactory way of talking about God, is to point out that Ivan has made no mention of the man who in his innocence took great suffering upon himself—Christ. Ivan, however, has not forgotten Christ: his reply is his 'poem'. Alyosha shall be his 'first reader—that is, listener'.

It is set in sixteenth-century Seville 'in the most terrible time of the Inquisition, when fires were lighted every day to the glory of God, and "in the splendid *auto da fé* the wicked heretics are burnt" ' (p. 295). Ivan visualizes the return of Christ and although 'he came softly, unobserved', walking amongst the crowds he is immediately recognized. The response is like that of the crowds at the height of his Galilean ministry. As then, he heals, but he is silent. The Cardinal, the Grand Inquisitor, appears, and observes.

He knits his thick grey brows and his eyes gleam with a sinister fire. He holds out his finger and bids the guards take him. And such is his power, so completely are the people cowed into submission and trembling obedience to him, that the crowd immediately make way for the guards, and in the midst of deathlike silence they lay hands on Him and lead Him away. (p. 296)

Late that night the Inquisitor comes to his cell and there ensues a long monologue in which the Inquisitor offers both a justification of himself and an indictment of Christ and his teaching.

The burden of his charge against the Christ is stated as follows:

Thou didst think too highly of men . . . for they are slaves, of course, though rebellious by nature. Look around and judge; fifteen centuries have passed, look upon them. Whom hast thou raised up to Thyself? I swear, man is weaker and baser by nature than thou has believed him. . . . By showing him so much respect, thou didst as it were, cease to feel for him, for thou didst ask far too much from him—. . . Respecting him less, thou wouldst have asked less of him. That would have been more like love, for his burden would have been lighter. (p. 304)

The Inquisitor and his allies have taken upon themselves to recognize the weakness of men and to correct and complete the work which Christ began. This, however, is at the price of taking from the mass of men and women their freedom. In the end, men are unable to bear the gift of freedom and in return for their freedom, the Inquisitor offers them happiness. In the temptations in the wilderness, he points out, Christ rejected all that could have given him the power to make men happy. He refused to satisfy human hunger by bread made out of stones: he refused the temptation of the spectacular, the diverting, the miraculous leap from the pinnacle of the temple; finally he refused to accept the authority of earthly power, the authority which could be his if he had bowed down to his temptor and chosen the sword of Caesar to use it for good.

Instead of these ways to the hearts of men Christ preferred to leave men free to respond to him. Instead of miracle, mystery and authority, with which the Inquisitor sets about 'correcting' his work, Christ has left to men all that is 'exceptional, enigmatic and vague'.

In place of the rigid ancient law, man must hereafter with free heart decide for himself what is good and what is evil, having only thy image before him as guide (p. 302).

Such a burden is too great for the many. For the few perhaps, for the strong, it is adequate.

But they only were some thousands; and what of the rest? And how are the other weak ones to blame, because they could not endure what the strong have endured? How is the weak soul to blame that it is unable to receive such terrible gifts? Canst thou have simply come *to* the elect and *for* the elect? . . . fifteen centuries have passed, look upon them.

Who is it that loves men? Christ who gives to the many a freedom which the many find intolerable? As the Inquisitor points out, those who that day

kissed thy feet, to-morrow at the faintest sign from me will rush to heap up the embers of thy fire (p. 297).

Or is it the Inquisitor who gives to the many both bread and the security which they want (or is it 'need'?), who loves men the most? He and the few, are willing to bear the burden of the knowledge of good and evil, to knowingly choose the way which Christ rejected, and to deceive the people while feeding them, 'declaring falsely that it is in thy name' (p. 300).

The tale ends thus:

When the Inquisitor ceased speaking he waited some time for the Prisoner to answer him. His silence weighed down upon him. He saw that the Prisoner had listened intently all the time, looking gently in his face and evidently not wishing to reply. The old man longed for him to say something, however bitter and terrible. But he suddenly approached the old man in silence and softly kissed him on his bloodless aged lips. That was all his answer. The old man shuddered. His lips moved. He went to the door, opened it, and said to him: 'Go, and come no more . . . come not at all, never, never!' (p. 311)

These are some of the main elements of this puzzling disturbing tale.


## II


At the beginning of the fourth chapter of Book V Ivan confesses to Alyosha that he never could understand 'how one can love one's neighbours'. He suggests that this is not a problem about what love in general is, and charity to the anonymous beggar seems to afford him no theoretical difficulties. To say the least, this is a rather contentious and perhaps deliberately inconsequential way of introducing one of the central problems of the novel, and as such it is quite in keeping with what we already know of Ivan. It is as if love in general raised no great problems; but one perhaps relatively minor form of love—of one's neighbour—did trouble him somewhat. In typical fashion, however, the lens of his emotions and intellect very quickly focuses upon love of one's neighbour and magnifies that image to fill our field of attention.

To my thinking, Christ-like love for men is a miracle impossible on earth. He was God. But we are not Gods.

At this point all mention of Christ incarnate disappears, and theodicy becomes the target of his polemic. His discussion of theodicy, however, is not a discussion of some of the standard ways of calling theodicy into question. The omnipotence of God is not denied: there is no dualistic hypothesis offered in its place. Nor is what philosophers now refer to as 'the free-will defence', discussed.

Ivan's rejection of those patterns of argument has already been analysed. We have euclidean minds. Ivan's doubts are not about what a God who is omnipotent could or could not do: he does not enter into the argument concerning whether or not an omnipotent God could so create men that they always freely choose to do what is good.[7] For Ivan that is not the crucial issue. Perhaps it is impossible for an omnipotent God to bring about the logically possible state of affairs that all men freely choose to do what is good. Perhaps, that is to say, the free-will defence is based on sound arguments. Ivan's questions however, do not relate to either the omnipotence of God, or the omniscience of God, they relate to the love of God for his creation. He is, in a sense, prepared to accept God, but, what of God's creation? His returning of the ticket is a refusal to accept that this world is both a creation of God, and expressive of the love of God. The argument of Chapter IV, Book V could be paraphrased as 'If this world is the expression of the love of God for man, what hopes can one hold out for the love of man for man?' Even if Christ is God, there is little indication that the love of Christ for men is possible, in earth *or* heaven.

Chapter V, 'The Grand Inquisitor', brings the argument, at Alyosha's prompting, back to Christ the man, back also to Ivan's insistence that 'Christ-like love for men is a miracle impossible here on earth'. The question which Ivan sets in Chapter IV is whether this impossibility is due to 'men's bad qualities', or whether it is due to something 'inherent in their nature'. Is it because men so choose, that there is moral evil, or is it that what looks like moral evil is in fact simply a consequence of the nature of man—a reflection of that nature, caused rather than chosen? The tale of the Grand Inquisitor brings a new possibility into the picture: perhaps much human suffering is not *despite* Christ's gift of love to men—freedom; perhaps this gift itself is, because of what it is, 'a burden too great to bear', and hence a source of pain rather than happiness. Is love of one's neighbour possible? If so, on what terms? It is with this question in Chapter IV that Ivan and Dostoyevsky forewarn us of the interrogation to which 'a senseless poem of a senseless student' will subject us in Chapter V.

In religious terms, then, Ivan's poem is essentially a study of Christ, but, it is a study of Christ consequent upon a rejection of belief in God. Guardini reminds us that this Christ is the imaginative creation of an atheist and it is as well to be clear about this at the outset. We are offered a humanistic and atheistic picture of Christ and of Christianity, described in the Inquisitor's words as follows:

In place of the rigid ancient law, man must hereafter with free heart decide for himself what is good and what is evil, having only thy image before him as guide.

There is no mention here of God, or providence, or of the third person of the trinity. The gift of freedom leaves no room in this conception for grace or for the activity of God underlying and supporting the activity of men. It is this aspect of Ivan's thought that attracted the interest of the self-styled 'death-of-God' writers in the 1960s. In his essay 'Banished from the Land of Unity',[8] William Hamilton, both caught and misrepresented this aspect of Ivan's state of mind when he insisted

It was not that he (Ivan) decided to deny God and choose man and his freedom, but that he wanted to be a theologian without a theodicy.[9]

This may have been true of Dostoyevsky, and to this we shall return in the final chapter, but it certainly was not true of Ivan. Nor, however, is the view rejected by Hamilton adequate: Ivan's 'acceptance' of freedom is at best ambivalent, as, of course, despite Hamilton, is his 'acceptance' of God.

There is nothing to suggest that Ivan's Christ is an emissary from, let alone an incarnation of, a transcendent omnipotent active God, about whom we may speculate. He offers no authoritative word for men, no final judgement of the Inquisitor. All that he offers is some sort of freedom, freedom, it is alleged, to decide what is good and what is evil. Miracle, mystery, and authority have been left behind, and belief in God seems to have been replaced by a faith in the potentialities of men and women to accept and to respond to this gift of freedom. It is important to note in passing that this Christ has nothing to say, literally or figuratively about the suffering of children. It would be reading too much into the enigmatic kiss with which he responds to the Inquisitor, to see that clearly as a comment on the oppressor, even if it says little to comfort the oppressed.

Whatever the literary elegance of the conclusion to the tale, George Steiner characterizes one's discomfort admirably.

From the philosophical point of view, it has about it something of evasion. [10]

Whether in Book VI Dostoyevsky can give 'a sufficient answer' is yet to be discussed.

Hamilton argues that Ivan, like Karl Barth in his *Romans*[11] wants a theology without a theodicy: it could be said of Hamilton, that he and some of his fellow radicals wished to retain the option of belief by looking for a Christology without a theology. Ivan would have been happy with neither of these. It has been argued by many, including Berdyaev, that Ivan's poem is a vindication of Christ, and it is from such view as this, perhaps, that the death-of-God lobby took heart. The fundamental error of such a view is twofold: (a) it assumes that the picture given of the Grand Inquisitor is wholly antipathetic; and (b) that the endorsement of the value and potential of freedom is wholehearted. It is in the false light of these two assumptions that many of Dostoyevsky's commentators have made artificial hay. Those who deduce from the Legend reactionary anti-socialist views, and unalloyed trust in the powers of human freedom are less than thorough in their reading of Ivan's tale, whatever may be true of the tenor of Dostoyevsky's journalistic *Diary of a Writer*.

The Inquisitor's primary question to Christ is about the nature of love. His way of life, whatever it has become, was initially an expression of compassion for those

millions and tens of thousands of millions of creatures who will not have the strength to forego the earthly bread for the sake of the heavenly.

The critique of utopianism which is certainly here, is not simply an early or primitive version of Huxley's *Brave New World* or Orwell's *Nineteen Eighty-Four*, for these give us monochrome pictures of the utopia-builders: they are the social engineers and power-seekers devoid of humanity and compassion. The Inquisitor is not empty of either. He embodies that aspect of all of us which wants to 'help others who cannot help themselves'. Ivan identifies the source of his activity for us as a moment of moral insight:

All his life he loved humanity, and suddenly his eyes were opened, and he saw that it is no great moral blessedness to attain perfection and freedom, if at the same time one gains the conviction that millions of God's creatures have been created as a mockery, that they will never be capable of using their freedom (p. 310).

Ivan's insistence is that there are moral questions to be raised about the gift of freedom: Is it always an expression of love and compassion? To the freewill defence, Ivan raises the intelligible and thus legitimate question: 'Even if freedom is a gift of God which makes it clear how it is possible that the innocent can suffer in the interests of a higher harmony, is such a gift the expression of love? The focus here is not, as in the earlier chapter, upon those who suffer from the malevolent exercise of freedom by the powerful: the focus is rather upon the recipients of this gift. Again the focus is not upon the gift of freedom as a choice between doing what we know to be good, or alternatively what we know to be evil: the gift of freedom discussed here is the more radical freedom to decide what is to count as good and what is to count as evil. In Ivan's picture, we are not posed with the question of whether to respond in some way to the love of Christ: we are faced with the question of whether a radically antinomian Christ is a Christ of love.

Ivan is thus countering two possible replies to his discussion of the suffering of children. Initially his poem is directed towards the introduction of Christ into the argument: at a secondary level he is rejecting the appeal to freedom, and the gift of freedom as adequate justification for the suffering which it brings with it—suffering, that is to say, to the recipients of the gift. Who loves men? Christ or the Inquisitor? The Inquisitor came to believe the gift of freedom to be too great for the many, the weak, to bear, and consequently rejected it:

frenzied efforts to subdue his flesh to make himself free and perfect. But yet all his life he loved humanity and suddenly his eyes were opened, and he saw that it is no great moral blessedness to attain perfection and freedom, if at the same time one gains a conviction that millions of God's creatures have been created as a mockery, that they will never be capable of using their freedom . . . . (p. 310)

In his chapter titled 'Freedom', Berdyaev attributes to Dostoyevsky a single-mindedness about freedom and its ultimate value which this section of the novel belies. The trust placed by Dostoyevsky, from *Notes from the Underground* to the *Diary of a Writer*, in the redemptive powers of human freedom is here the subject of the Inquisitor's penetrating gaze. Certainly his compassion for men becomes cynicism about the weakness of the mass of humanity, but for all that his early questions remain in need of answers.

The questions raised about Christ's gift of freedom are initially raised in the name of morality: is this a gift of love? They become, however, questions in the name of realism. This aspect of the Inquisitor's monologue is easily turned aside or ignored, by seeing only cynicism and from the standpoint of the twentieth century, the horrors to which the cynicism of the power-seekers has given rise. Dostoyevsky's question in the name of realism is subtly different from that of a self-seeking cynic. The Inquisitor simply reminds Christ:

. . . fifteen centuries have passed, look upon them. Whom hast thou raised up to Thyself?

Even if one does not wholly accept his diagnosis of the, at least apparent, impotence of the gift of this Christ figure, that 'man is weaker and baser by nature than thou hast believed him', one of the hardest questions for Christianity to answer remains: What difference has it made to the world of the many? For Dostoyevsky this is also a question about whether the inner freedom of which he had written elsewhere, is, and has been, as ubiquitous as he believed.

The third form given to Dostoyevsky's inquiry about the nature of Christ's gift is a recognition of some further facts about freedom. The world of the Inquisitor plainly reminds us that freedom can be taken from men. This is true not only of the external constraints which the Inquisitor and his ilk can put upon the lives of men, but as in their various ways Huxley, Orwell, and contemporary despots have shown us, men may have their capacity to think and believe as they wish, systematically engineered out of them. The romantic image of internal freedom of belief and conscience retained through rack and flame is simply out of date. Equally insistent is the Inquisitor's claim that for many, such is not necessary, for they are prepared to barter their freedom for bread, for a community which is single-minded about its absolutes, and for security. There are always those for whom the despots bring a welcome easing of the burden of freedom, whether that burden be hunger, uncertainty or anxiety.

Thus, in response to the initial dilemma of Chapter IV as to whether the difficulty in imagining Christ-like love here on earth is because of what we are, or because of what love is, Ivan's tale implies that both of these explanations are relevant. Christ-like love, the Inquisitor argues, demands too much of men, and it does so because its essence is the gift of a freedom which is a source of suffering rather than happiness. Just as the love of Christ as God is rejected in Chapter IV, so in Chapter V, this most human of Christs is found to give no convincing argument for the possibility of love between men: not because we cannot quite emulate that love, but because we must ask whether indeed he is a Christ of love. This is, of course, also to raise a question about the nature of love, a question which still exercised Dostoyevsky as much in the portrayal of Ivan and Alyosha, as it had in the relationship of Sonia to Raskolnikov.

These questions about the nature of love and its compatibility with Christ's gift of freedom leave a much more ambivalent picture of Christ than that claimed, for example, by Paul Ramsey,

At its deepest level, 'The Grand Inquisitor' proposes a solution to the problem of suffering in the terms in which it has been set forth. Christ is the one who suffers, in all and for all, all the suffering there has been under the sun; and so he alone is in a position—as the mother is not—to forgive the torturer, not only for the immeasurable suffering of his own heart but also for the suffering of the other innocents.[12]

As has been suggested, this is to imagine an Inquisitor who is completely without redeeming features, and a Christ who is much more than 'exceptional, enigmatic and vague'. It is also to ignore Dostoyevsky's own claim that his 'answer' to Ivan, and to atheism will be offered in Book VI.[13] Philip Rahv's account of the figure of Christ in Ivan's poem penetrates much more deeply the tensions in Ivan's psyche. He argues that in his poem, Ivan does not dispute the ideality and supreme goodness of Christ,

On the contrary, it is this very ideality and supreme goodness that he turns into the motive of his dissent when he depicts the Grand Inquisitor upbraiding Christ for thinking much too highly of man in endeavouring to augment his freedom of choice between good and evil instead of heeding the counsel of the wise and dread spirit of the wilderness to strip man of his freedom so that he might at long last live in peace and brutish happiness.[14]

As he adds,

The very manner in which Ivan develops this ideology expresses his loathing of it as he despairingly accepts it.[15]

In Chapter II it was argued that Ivan 'accepts' God, but in accepting, he rebels and rejects the possibility of God. In his poem there is a further acceptance and rejection, but at a deeper, and more desperate level. He accepts and rejects, Christian morality, accepts and rejects what Rahv calls the Grand Inquisitor's 'ideology'. Here, however, his despair comes to the point of definition. Whereas in his acceptance of God, humour, albeit dark humour, is involved, here the humour is revealed to be what Zossima diagnosed it to be: a mask, or a delaying tactic. Ivan's despairing perceptions made both more precise and yet more grotesque by the polar extremities which they represent, leave him without 'something to live by'.

The discussion of atheism in Book V Chapter V extends into a more general discussion of the nature of Christianity, of freedom, and of the possibility of loving one's neighbours. In so doing Dostoyevsky prefigures many of the enduring theological and philosophical debates of the twentieth century. It also embeds these discussions even more deeply into the psyche of one of his characters. As such Dostoyevsky has drawn the discussion of this essay further from the more general analysis of the nature of atheism which is correctly the primary focus of theological and philosophical discussion with which our discussion of Ivan began, and he has directed our attention more firmly to the particular literary outworking of this analysis in the mind and heart of an individual character. There is no firm boundary within the novel at which this transformation comes about, for the division in question belongs to discussion *of* the novel. Within that discussion there is such a boundary area, albeit far from precisely defined. Ivan is Dostoyevsky's portrayal of the outworking of these ideas. Many believers have seized upon his despair as Dostoyevsky's 'answer' to his atheism. In doing so they are far from the truth. Ivan's despair is undoubtedly a challenge to atheism and unbelief, but it is certainly not a refutation of them. Perhaps, however, it is a way of asking how far 'the facts', are like the Christ-figure's 'freedom'—for 'the strong', 'the few', rather than for the many. Many writers in the twentieth century have taken this challenge seriously and have attempted to give a portrayal of atheism which 'men can live by'. *Ivan*'s despair is particular, it belongs to Ivan: it is not universal, in so far at it is not an inevitable concomitant of rejection of belief. Dostoyevsky's 'answer' to atheism does not lend itself to the move of a dubious religious apologetic which justifies belief by pointing to Ivan's madness, and it is to Dostoyevsky's 'answer' that we must now turn.

## NOTES

[1] N. Berdyaev, *Dostoevsky* (Meridian Books, 1957), p. 188.

[2] R. Guardini, p. 64.

[3] Op. cit., p. 188.

[4] Steiner, p. 340.

[5] Rahv, p. 256.

[6] In more cynical moments one might derive some amusement from devising a competition for the award of prizes for the interpretation of the Legend of the Grand Inquisitor under various headings —Most ingeniously wrong, most blatantly absurd, most trendy etc. Certainly a candidate under one of those headings ought to be A. H. Maslow who in his *Religions, Values and Peak-Experiences* (Viking Compass Books, 1970), p. 25 finds in the Grand Inquisitor a 'classical' statement of the way in which those 'who rise to the top in any complex bureaucracy tend to be non-peakers rather than peakers'!

[7] As for example does Alvin Plantinga in *God and Other Minds*, ch. 6, where he discusses the views of A. Flew and J. L. Mackie.

[8] Reprinted in *Radical Theology and the Death of God*, eds. T. J. J. Altizer and W. Hamilton.

[9] Ibid., p. 64.

[10] *Tolstoy or Dostoevsky*, p. 342.

[11] K. Barth, *The Epistle to The Romans* (O.U.P., 1933).

[12] P. Ramsey, p. 33.

[13] See chapters VI–VII below also Dostoyevsky's letter to his editor quoted in ch. VI, pp. 82–3.

[14] P. Rahv, p. 252.

[15] Ibid., p. 253.

# VI
## 'An Artistic Picture'

The answer is presented as the direct opposite to the view of the world stated earlier—but again not presented point by point, but as an artistic picture, so to speak.

If in Book V Dostoyevsky devoted his energies to giving a portrayal of atheism, so in Book VI his hope was to provide an 'answer to' or 'refutation of' 'all those atheistical propositions'. The problems which faced Dostoyevsky here are both literary and philosophical. In literary terms the question is, How to proceed? What form should the next section of the novel take? Philosophically, the problem is that of the nature of the argument which may take place between belief and unbelief. Granted Ivan's exposition of the nature of atheism, is there a logically appropriate response which faith may make? The intention of this chapter is to examine the appropriateness of Dostoyevsky's response. He does sometimes speak as if we need look only to Book VI if we are to find the answer to Ivan's atheism, but elsewhere he does refer to the *whole* novel as 'giving answer'. If we are to make sense of this latter point, we must first, I suggest, find in Book VI our understanding of what is, for Dostoyevsky, to *count* as an answer.

Between the appearance of Books V and VI, Dostoyevsky gave some account of what he had attempted in the sixth book. In a letter to a trusted and valued friend he spoke of both his aims and his uncertainties:

Your opinion of what you have read of the Karamazovs (as to the power and energy of what I have written) was very flattering, but at that point you pose the *most pressing* problem: that I have not yet given answer to all those atheistical propositions, and that it must be done. Exactly so, and in this all my care and anxiety now reside. For the sixth book, 'A Russian Monk', which will appear on August 31st, is intended as the answer to all that *negative side.* And so I tremble for it in this sense: will it be a *sufficient* answer? Especially as the answer is not in fact direct, not an answer point by point to the theses previously expressed (in 'The Grand Inquisitor' and earlier), but only by implication. It is presented as the direct opposite of the view of the world stated earlier — but again not presented point by point, but as an artistic picture so to speak. This is what disturbs me, i.e. will it be understood, and shall I achieve even a part of my aim? And there was a further obligation of art: I had to present a modest but august figure, while life itself is full of the comic, and august only in its interior significance, so that in the biography of my monk I was forced, willy-nilly, by the demands of art, to touch on the commonplace and the trivial, so as not to mar artistic realism. Then there are several elements in the monk's teaching which will make people simply cry out that they are absurd because they are too high-flown. Of course they are absurd in the everyday sense, but in another, inward sense I think they are justified.[1]

In this quotation Dostoyevsky shows himself well aware that his problem was methodological as well as substantive. In his view the appropriate way to continue the discussion is not in terms of a point by point counter-argument but in the presentation of 'an artistic picture, so to speak'. The literary problem of how to proceed is attacked by literary and artistic means — with all the consequent implications of 'the obligations and demands of art', and of 'artistic realism'. Dostoyevsky did not move towards a more distinctively *philosophical* literary form in his attempt to solve the literary problem: he did not adopt the form of a philosophical dialogue — whether Socratic or Humean — nor of a philosophical treatise, thinly disguised as a series of speeches issuing from one or other of the characters. This left the residual worry that a literary solution to his problem would fail to achieve his purpose: his fear was that his artistic picture would not be 'a sufficient answer'. The judgement of many literary critics is that it is not a sufficient answer — that Book VI *is* a failure.

Such a judgement could be based on at least two different sorts of argument. On the one hand, it could be argued that Dostoyevsky simply fails in terms of his own stated aims: he does not succeed in presenting 'an artistic picture'. On the other hand, a much more fundamental question can be raised: Is there any reason to think that 'an artistic picture' can help settle a philosophical question such as that raised by Ivan concerning the significance of the language of religion. The argument here is that whether or not Dostoyevsky was

successful in 'literary' or 'artistic' terms, such success has little relevance to Ivan. It is an argument which has been deployed at least
since Plato suggested, in the *Republic*, that there would be no place
for poets in the city: a fundamental question of belief, even of
knowledge, is raised, and by way of an answer the artist— in this case
Dostoyevsky — offers us images — sights and sounds, products of
the imagination even further from truth and reality than the study of
historical examples.

The relationship between artistic or literary success and philosophical adequacy is a topic which can provide generalizations
sufficient to inflate many balloons, but this does not deter me from
hoping in due course to offer some specific suggestions about the
relationship between the two possible suggested grounds for regard-
ing Book VI as a failure. The main issue of this chapter, however, is
the question of whether or not 'an artistic picture, so to speak', could
be a philosophically adequate response to Ivan's atheism. More
bluntly, how could a piece of fiction possibly help resolve a
philosophical argument?

In fact, there are many ways in which this might happen, but I shall
restrict myself here to the particular example confronting us— Book
VI of *The Brothers Karamazov*. It should be noted, however, that to
argue that fiction can be philosophically important, that Dostoyevsky's *method* of continuing the argument by 'an artistic picture' is not
misguided, is not necessarily to argue that the project has been successfully carried out. What the detailed discussion of the *philosophical* importance of a specific piece of fiction *can* provide is a set
of criteria which will be relevant to assessing whether or not in
*literary* terms the passage in question succeeds or fails.

The dispute between Ivan, and his brother Alyosha, the novitiate
monk and disciple of Zossima, is a dispute about whether or not
what Ivan calls 'a Euclidean mind' can see in the language of religion,
sense or significance beyond that which is trivial or morally unacceptable. Ivan's argument is that such expressions as 'God', 'worship', 'eternal life', 'miracle', 'prayer', and so on, are either used as he
has outlined, or they are used to produce nonsense.

One could imagine a certain sort of atheist or agnostic making at
least two different kinds of comments about Zossima, as he is
portrayed throughout Books I to VI, but particularly in Book VI. He
might say, (a) How queer that anyone should live like that; or, I can't
understand how anyone could live like that, I can't see the point of it

all. Or he might say, (b) What strange things he says, for example, that 'everyone is responsible for everyone else', or that, 'if you love everything, you will see the divine mystery in things', or, 'I just can't understand what he says'; or more strongly 'he talks nonsense'. Clearly in the second case the questions being raised concern the concepts of meaning or sense, issues about the meaning or sense of some of the expressions which Zossima uses. On one philosophical view one might argue that the former set of questions are quite unconnected with the latter. On this view one might argue that whether or not those expressions and the various others which seem to belong to the language of religion have sense or meaning depends upon a matter of objective fact: Does God exist, or does he not? If reality, if the inventory of things or persons in the real world includes God, then these expressions may have a meaning or sense which may be derived from that fact. Until Dostoyevsky addresses himself to this question, 'artistic picture' or not, all talk of 'refuting' Ivan is misguided. The view that Ivan's atheism can best be understood as simply the negation of the proposition 'God exists' has been rejected in Chapter II above. If the analysis of atheism presented there stands, then, it will not be an adequate response to Ivan, simply to try to establish that the inventory of things or persons in the world includes one additional item to which the name 'God' is attached.

An alternative philosophical view would be to connect the two sorts of remarks, (a) and (b) in the following way: I can't understand what he says because I can't see what distinction is marked by saying, 'Everyone is responsible for everyone else', or 'If you love everything you will see the divine mystery in things': I can't see what difference it makes to utter these sounds rather than not utter them at all. If someone were to say, 'The cost of living is higher in France than it is in the United Kingdom', or, 'When you go to university study economics rather than literature', then I can see what difference it makes to say the one thing rather than the other. I know what implications may be drawn from such assertions and exhortations, and also what sorts of reasons are appropriate to their acceptance or rejection. The problem with utterances of the sort made by Zossima is that it is difficult, if not impossible, to give a coherent account of the differences which these utterances mark in the pattern of Zossima's life.

Consider now the following remarks by Wittgenstein:

*Zettel* 263. Hence there is something right about saying that unimaginability is a criterion for nonsensicality.

*Zettel* 247. For what does it mean: 'to discover that a sentence does not make sense'?

And what does this mean: 'if I mean something by it, surely it must make sense'?

The first presumably means: not to be misled by the appearance of a sentence and to investigate its application in the language-game.

And 'if I mean something by it' — does that mean something *like*: 'if I can imagine something in connection with it'? — An image often leads on to a further application.

*Investigations* 19.    . . . And to imagine a language means to imagine a form of life.

My contention is that there is a very close parallel between the sense of these remarks and Dostoyevsky's actual procedure when faced with a fundamental dispute as to whether a range of terms had meaning or significance or whether, alternatively, the language of religion was either nonsensical, or confined to playing a trivial role in the lives of men. I am not concerned to argue whether or not there was an historical influence of the one upon the other, but it is of interest to note that Wittgenstein did know well, and have high regard for, *The Brothers Karamazov*, and particularly for the figure of Zossima.[2]

What is at stake in the question of whether expressions like 'God' and 'eternal life' do have the sense which Ivan denied to them, is whether or not these expressions and our use of them can be 'connected' to one another and to a whole range of other terms, i.e. do they belong to a language? If they do, then one can imagine what that language is, how it functions, what is the range of connections open to these terms within that language. To imagine a language, however, as Wittgenstein points out, is much more than imagining a series of sounds or ciphers: it is to imagine a form of life, and this, I suggest is an alternative account of what Dostoyevsky is doing in offering 'an artistic picture, so to speak', instead of 'an answer point by point to the theses previously expressed'. He is imagining a form of life. He is attempting to show the significance of the language and practice of religion by showing how the various expressions peculiar to religious language may be connected to one another, and how in these interconnections they bear on the sense which terms not peculiar to the language of religion have. Thus, for example, in the artistic picture we see how in Zossima's life terms such as 'responsibility', 'guilt', 'freedom', 'justice', 'a man' came to play roles quite different from the role which they had in the lives of many of his contemporaries. In being shown what roles they do play, what differences are marked, what behaviour is appropriate to talk of 'preserving the image of Christ', 'the spiritual dignity of man', 'praying to God for gladness', we are being shown the sense which these expressions have. If one can thus imagine the connections, imagine the language and the form of life, one has established what sense the language of religion has. If it is other than the sense which Ivan has permitted, then he has, to that extent been answered.

At this point, however, a more detailed discussion is required of what is, or could be meant by 'imagining a form of life'. Although many contemporary philosophers have been happy to use Wittgenstein's notion of a form of life. There has been little discussion of, as distinct from appeal to, the idea.

The notion of imagining a form of life is by no means as clear as Wittgenstein seems to have thought, and the account which follows is tentative in nature, though it will, I hope, open up the issues. What is presented is certainly not intended as an exposition of Wittgenstein, but rather an attempt to use more systematically an expression to be found in his writings. I have discussed elsewhere the extent to which his account of 'a form of life' is not clear and unified and I have considerable doubts about the compatibility of what follows with all of the various remarks to be found in Wittgenstein about a 'form of life'. To this extent at least, I am stipulating how the expression will be used throughout the rest of this essay. Of the four uses of the expression listed by J. F. M. Hunter in his paper ' "Forms of Life" in Wittgenstein's *Philosophical Investigations*',[3] my use is nearest to the one which he rejects as the least plausible interpretation of the *Investigations*, viz. the view that a form of life is a way of life. The attempt then by Dostoyevsky to portray a form of life is the attempt to show us the way in which Zossima strives to live. By using the expression 'form of life' I wish to draw attention to the fact that if he is to succeed in his aim, Dostoyevsky's 'artistic picture' must show that there is a form of life of which religion as practised by Zossima is a part, and that such a form of life provides a framework of sufficient diversity *and* coherence, that it is possible to talk of Zossima as having 'something to live by' in which the religious expressions and practices play both a distinctive and integrating role.

By 'form' or 'way' of life I intend partially to talk about an ideal of coherence and comprehensiveness which few of us ever approach, but which for many informs their fitful attempts to achieve a measure of the wholeness and consistency of integrity in how they live. Dostoyevsky is, in his artistic picture, attempting to show that it is possible for the language and practises of religion to be a part of such a wholeness and consistency. Indeed, in the way of life which he tries to depict, religious beliefs and practice play a central distinctive role. The demands of wholeness here are such that many different aspects of human deeds and institutions are potential focuses of inquiry. Thus one can in principle ask a very wide range of questions of Dostoyevsky's artistic picture: e.g. How do Zossima's religious beliefs relate to the scientific or political views of his contemporaries?; What bearing do they have on traditional Russian Orthodoxy?; or, Would his way of life involve rejection of particular types of economic activity or educational practices? and so on. These questions could arise in an attempt to clarify what way of life is being portrayed here. On the other hand, granted that we are dealing with a way of life, which questions are important ones will be determined in any particular discussion by the alternative ways of life with which this one is being compared. For example, a man for whom the institutions of liberal democracy have a fundamental value or importance would be inclined to focus discussion upon the role which these institutions might or might not have within the form of life to which Zossima's religion belongs. The acceptability of a form of life within which these particular religious practices have the central role which they do would be partially determined for that man by such an inquiry.

The context given in the novel, of course, dictates which questions will be central for this discussion: What is the difference between speculation and belief?; What account of the nature of love can be given? What is the role of the emotions in religious belief? and most crucial of all, Can the form of life in question give a possible response to evil and suffering, which involves neither despair nor moral abdication? These are the issues of comprehensiveness or wholeness which, through Ivan's questions, Dostoyevsky has made central to the attempt in Book VI to offer us 'an artistic picture'.

The form of life then is not simply the sum of religious beliefs and practices. Producing a self-consistent set of these need not raise major difficulties, but it could have the limitations of an esoteric game. Nor is the form of life to be understood as simply an attitude or set of attitudes to the world, for these attitudes could be inconsistent with other beliefs, and lack comprehensiveness or wholeness in the manner in which they enable us to come to terms with the world in which we live. Nor, however, should the form of life be equated simply with a series of idiosyncratic responses or reactions to that world, for these responses, if isolated from all else that belongs to a form of life, could amount to no more than the refusal of the superstitious to walk under ladders. Of course, the religious beliefs and practices, the attitudes and the reactions, each of these may play a part within particular forms of life, and even help make the ways of life in question distinctive, but they do not individually or even collectively, constitute a form of life.

One of the problems involved is giving a clear account of just what may and what may not count as a 'form of life'. What can constitute a way of life? There are no final criteria here, and I do not understand what it would mean to specify in advance criteria which could delineate the form of all possible forms of life. This does not leave the situation, however, completely arbitrary, for we are able to rule out certain accounts as *not* depicting a form of life. There are clearly two general ways in which an account can so fail: one is when what one is depicting simply could not under any description, no matter how accurate, detailed, or sympathetic, count as a form or way of life, e.g. the description of the random and arbitrary actions of someone afflicted with severe brain disorder; the second is when one's account fails through faulty description of one sort or another, and as we shall see, descriptions can be defective in a number of different ways. One problem which does arise in certain cases, however, is that of deciding in the case of failure, whether the defect can be attributed to the description, or to some defect in the contemplated way of life. We shall return to this later.

One point already clear from an example considered earlier is that imagining a form of life is much more than simply listing some observable behaviour differences between that form of life and another. Such differences are amongst the materials which go to make up the description of a form of life but by themselves they are insufficient, just as an account af Picasso's charcoal drawing of Don Quixote in terms of an enumeration of the various lines which go to make up the drawing would be insufficient. The trouble with such a description is that we should not be able to draw any inferences which could lead us beyond the description in question. We might be able to work out from the description that there was a very high likelihood of the words 'Let us pray' being followed by everyone kneeling and closing their eyes, but this would at most be parallel to the force which Hume allowed to our causal inferences, the previous constant conjunction of these three observables. We could not on any reckoning be said to have given an account of a form of life of which prayer is a part.

Nor will it be sufficient, as Peter Winch points out,[4] to restrict one's account to

the logical coherence of the rules according to which activities are carried out . . . For . . . there comes a point where we are not even in a position to determine what is and what is not coherent in such a context of rules, without raising questions about the point which following those rules has. . . .

To appeal to the same example, it is only when one knows something of the point of prayer and worship that one can see that there is something incoherent in beginning a prayer with the words 'I thank thee that I am not as other men are'. Someone who did pray in these terms would, amongst other things, be victim of a very serious misunderstanding of the nature and point of prayer within the Christian tradition. The issue at stake here is the issue of what can count as coherent or incoherent: we cannot foreclose the inquiry by assuming that the criteria of coherence or incoherence which apply within other forms of life will apply here too. Rather then than *assume* an account of coherence and incoherence, we must find out what standards of coherence and incoherence are operating within the form of life in question. If there are no such standards to be found, then that is tantamount to saying that we are not dealing with a form of life.

Related distinctions which play a parallel central role in the elucidation of the notion of a form of life are those between truth and falsehood and between appearance and reality. I should not want to conflate these distinctions either with one another or with that between coherence and incoherence. Nor should I want the points I am making to be equated with appeal to a fairly crude form of the coherence theory of truth. This latter accusation would amount to the claim that for any proposed form of life to qualify as an accepted form of life it must embody a coherence theory of truth. On the contrary certain forms of life seem to me to be as they are to quite some considerable extent because they embody one form or other of the correspondence theory of truth. My point minimally is that a purported form of life must have implicit within it clear criteria of truth and falsehood if it is even to merit consideration as a form of life. Likewise a purported form of life must have within it *some*, at least *prima facie*, distinction between appearance and reality if it is to be considered as a serious candidate for acceptance as a form of life.

This immediately, or possibly on a second reading, ought to disqualify the sorts of excessive posturing or self-deception which many philosophers seem to fear could be given some sort of status merely by the *claim* that they amount to forms of life. It does also mean, however, that the examination of a series of patterns of linguistic and other activity which, it is thought, may amount to a form of life is not a matter for superficial inquiry. It does raise fundamental philosophical questions about the forms which the distinction between, for example, appearance and reality may take. Minimally, it is being argued that we cannot approach possible forms of life with one and only one permissible way of drawing this distinction. Alternatively, however, it is also being argued that not anything at all can count as a form of life. That a certain pattern does embody a distinction between appearance and reality must be shown. It cannot be assumed. Whether or not this can be shown will be a matter for inquiry and argument. The greater the difference between the form of life in question and the way in which we live, the longer and more complex the argument is likely to be. At least since the time of Socrates, however, that some philosophical arguments should be long and detailed has not been under dispute!

If we do talk of the logic implicit in a form of life, and of the standards of coherence and incoherence, we are talking about the possibility of drawing inferences from what is said and what is done. That is to say, we are talking about the connections which hold within that form of life. Imagining a form of life is then imagining what can go with this and this, imagining what is required to connect them. One important point here is that the connections which we find are not contingent connections: and the inferences which we are thereby enabled to draw are therefore not restricted to what is the case. We ought to be in a position to draw inferences about what might be the case, about how the form of life may develop or change. The latter, however, would not be in terms of a probability

prediction about how things may go, but rather in terms of an indication of what developments are *compatible with* this form of life:
what changes may be made without leading us to say that the form of
life in question has been abandoned or replaced by another. For
example if we have shown what the connections are operating within the form of life to which prayer and worship belong, we ought to
be able to draw inferences about what sorts of words may coherently
follow the injunction, 'Let us pray'. If the only inferences which we
may draw about whether a particular set of utterances may be part or
the whole of a prayer rest on asking whether we have so far encountered these utterances within what we take to be genuine examples of prayer, then we have not yet elicited the connections
which bind the various aspects of this way of life together. If we can
say of a particular utterance, 'No I have not heard anyone in prayer
say that, but I can quite well imagine that he should want to pray in
that way', then we have clearly begun to grasp the connections, to
understand 'the logical rules of coherence according to which the
activities are carried out'.

Linked to this point in a rather important way for a discussion of a
novel is the notion of 'filling out the picture'. Wittgenstein makes use
of this in

*Zettel* 252. 'I can quite well imagine someone acting like that and nevertheless seeing nothing shameful in the action.' There follows a description
showing how this is to be imagined. 'I can imagine a human society in
which it counts as dishonest to calculate, expect as a pastime.' That
means roughly the same as: I could easily fill this picture out with more
detail.

The procedure which Wittgenstein mentions here is not an arbitrary
procedure. One cannot fill out the picture in any way at all. The
belief that a man who calculates with any serious intent is dishonest
cannot belong in *any* sort of society: it cannot be connected with any
and every other sort of belief and practice indiscriminately. It could
only make sense to charge such a man with dishonesty in certain
well-defined contexts. That this is so is a matter of logic: one can only
infer the dishonesty of such practices given certain other beliefs and
circumstances. It could not follow from anything and within any
context that a man who calculates is dishonest. For one thing it is
necessary that the concepts of dishonesty and calculation be invested
with a sense which they do not possess within our society.

The earlier remark quoted here from *Zettel* 252, bears this out and also sheds some light on what George Steiner calls 'the paradox of the "independent character"'.[5] In view of the argument so far it should not surprise us to learn that some writers prefer to speak of their characters as, in some sense at least, independent of their creator. Tolstoy said of Vronsky in *Anna Karenina* at one point,

Vronsky, to my own amazement, tried to shoot himself!

The point is that having started to fill out the picture, and indeed having done so in some considerable detail, one is restricted in the inferences which one can draw. Not only is it the case that not anything can follow from what has gone before, sometimes one reaches the position where one can say, 'He could only . . .', where if the character is to act *consistently* then one, and only one, course of action can follow. These situations are rare, and if the character is to be both whole and convincing, are the product of genius, but they do throw into relief how a character may gain, indeed if the creation is to be successful, can only gain, a form of independence of its creator. This is inevitable in so far as it is the case that in creating his characters a writer sees them within, fills in the detail of, a form of life. In so doing he has committed both himself and his character to certain standards of coherence, to the possibility of some inferences and the rejection of others. Thus an objectivity must of necessity become part of the situation. If it does not then the author has been unsuccessful in presenting us with a living and convincing characterization.

If, without tedium, one additional example may be introduced, the range of *Zettel* 252 can be further explored. The example relates to the earlier remark: 'I can quite well imagine someone acting like that and nevertheless seeing nothing shameful in the action.' This remark makes obvious sense along with the rider, 'and in those circumstances I should see nothing shameful in it either'. The interesting cases, in the present context, however, are those in which this rider would not apply: that is, those where one would oneself still see something shameful in the action in question. One example would be where a convinced monogamist may be speaking of a polygamy practised in another culture, but one in which he would not wish to participate.

A further and even more pointed case is raised by Camus's novel *The Outsider*. There, Mersault does act in perhaps a number of ways which many readers would, and certainly the judge in Mersault's trial did, consider shameful. Clearly Mersault saw nothing shameful in a number of disputed instances, not least in his shooting of the Arab on the beach. On one interpretation of the novel, Camus is saying, and trying to teach the reader to say 'I can quite well imagine someone acting like that and seeing nothing shameful in the action.' To teach us how to say that, he must succeed in showing us what he claims he can imagine. Whether or not he succeeds will depend upon his ability to show us the inner connections which bind together the actions which we could only see as individually evocative of shame; and perhaps even more importantly to show us how these actions are connected to the other dimensions of Mersault's life. In short, the success of the novel depends, on this interpretation, on Camus's success in presenting us with a 'form of life'. If Camus succeeds we may have learned to regard Mersault as amoral rather than immoral: that is to say we regard his actions individually neither with praise nor condemnation, but as belonging to a different form of life from our own within which our own distinctions between good and evil do not apply. Whether or not the form of life *as such* may be subject to moral evaluation is a separate question which will reappear later. What is at stake at present, is that one could come to see here a possible form of life rather than a random collection of items and events. There would then exist a possible description of the death of the Arab in terms of Mersault's *actions and deeds* rather than in terms solely of events and happenings.[6]

Mention should be made of R. Rhees's paper *Wittgenstein's Builders* and I want now to outline two relevant points arising from it. Rhees argues that one of the difficulties which is to be found in Wittgenstein's use of the Builders to illustrate his claim that 'To imagine a language means to imagine a form of life', lies in imagining that the builders use their proposed rudimentary language only to give these few special orders. Rhees supports this particular conclusion by insisting upon the importance of expressions which are used within any one context having uses in other contexts as well:

Their uses elsewhere have to do with the point or bearing of them in what we are saying now. It is the way in which we have come to know them in other connections that decides whether it makes sense to put them together here, for instance: whether one can be substituted for another, whether they are incompatible and so forth. The meaning that they have within this game is not to be seen simply in what we do with them or how we react to them in this game.[7]

One of the points in stressing this feature of language is to bring out the distinction between an activity which is a part of a *game* and one which could be imagined as belonging to a *form of life*. To consider the activity of worship, the application of Rhees's point is that unless the expressions which belong here as part of the activity of worshipping have uses outside of that activity, then worship will turn out to be no more than a sophisticated game. The point of any movement or utterance will be wholly explicable in terms of the other movements or utterances: thus just as the significance of the umpire's raised forefinger is to be accounted for in terms of trajectory of the ball direct from the bat to the fieldsman's hands and the cry of, 'Howzat?', so the significance or point of the response, 'And our mouths shall show forth Thy praise' is to be shown in terms of the request, 'Open Thou our lips', and in terms of the posture of humility, belief in a transcendent God, and the form of life which goes with that belief. Unless the utterance which is part of formal worship has some sort of connection with what lies outside the worshipping situation, then the utterance can only have the significance of a move in a game.

A closely related though separate point concerns not just the significance of the utterance in the sense of the 'meaning' of the utterance. The point here is that the terms and expressions used in one context derive part of the sense which they have in that context from the sense which they have in others. In the article quoted, Rhees seems to take this point in a slightly stronger way than I should want to. He seems to argue that unless an expression is used in more than one context, more than one situation, it will never be more than a cipher in a game. I do not think that one has to go as far as this. It can quite well be imagined that a believer uses certain expressions for which some unbelievers have no use, e.g. 'God', 'prayer', 'worship', 'eternal life' and so on. He also uses certain expressions for which the unbeliever, and at times the believer, have a slightly different use, e.g. 'guilt', 'faith', 'belief', 'fear and trembling' and so on. Now the latter expressions fit Rhees's point, they have an obvious use in other, non-religious contexts, and the clear evidence for this is that the non-believer uses them.

The former set of expressions are, however, in a different class, but Rhees's point can be modified to apply to them in either of the following two ways: (1) These expressions must, if they are to be meaningful, have uses for the believer outside explicitly religious contexts. The word 'God' comes within this class. Unless the word has some uses outside the explicitly, and, one might add, 'formally' religious activities (e.g. worship and prayer) then it may well be reduced to being a cipher in a game, having no meaning, conveying no sense. That is to say: one way of deciding whether the word 'God' has meaning or sense is to consider whether in addition to addressing God in prayer and worship (i.e. using the word thus 'O God make speed to save us') we also have uses for the word in non-worshipping contexts, e.g. speaking of a particular event, or action as 'expressing the love of God'.

Alternatively (2): There are, it seems, certain words which belong implicitly and primarily to such contexts, e.g. those which name religious activities 'worship' or 'prayer', and those which may be used correctly solely to characterize God, e.g. 'ineffable', 'omniscient', and so on. The adaption of Rhees's point here is that although we may not have a use for these expressions outside of a religious context we none the less 'connect' these expressions with others which do have uses in such non-religious contexts, e.g. with the expression 'guilt', 'responsibility', 'love', 'judgement' and so on. Again only if we can establish or *show* such connections may we be sure that the expressions in question have sense or meaning, are other than ciphers in a game of some sort. I do not wish to imply here a reductionist view of religious language. Indeed I am not sure that the possibility of a reductionist view makes sense, depending as it does, on the view that we can give exhaustive accounts of the uses *and possible uses* of the terms in our language. I do not want to say that the meaning of the expression in question 'prayer', 'worship', 'ineffable', 'eternal', 'God' and so on, can be 'cashed without remainder' into scientific, empirical, moral, or any other terms. In fact the whole emphasis of this discussion points quite in the opposite direction. My point here, however, is to insist that there must be connections between religious and non-religious terms, between religious and non-religious contexts, and that the only alternative to a reductionist view is not a 'closed-shop' view.

*Conclusions*

In this section I have been attempting to clarify what account we may give of the logical status of Book VI of *The Brothers Karamazov*, and of the logical structure of the argument within it. In response to Ivan's challenge to belief Dostoyevsky has given us 'an artistic picture'. This, I have argued, is a particular response to Ivan's insistence upon the rejection of any other conception of God than that of the Russian boys. The problem had thus become one of giving or showing a possible sense of the language of belief which was other than the idolatrous, anthropomorphic sense allowed by Ivan.

By appealing to remarks from Wittgenstein's *Zettel* connecting the notions of sense and imaginability, and further, to some remarks about 'forms of life' I have attempted to show that Dostoyevsky is working on sound philosophical foundations. Book VI, on this view, is an attempt to imagine a form of life in which the language of religion has a part to play, i.e. does have a meaning and sense of its own. In one way, I am offering a definition of what Dostoyevsky means when he talks of offering to us 'an artistic picture, so to speak', by appealing to Wittgenstein's notion of 'imagining a form of life'. The next step in my argument is to quote a further part of the sentence in question from *Investigations*, thus:

To imagine a language means to imagine a form of life.

The conclusion which I wish to draw is that one of the fears felt by Dostoyevsky about the adequacy of the form of answer which he offers, need not trouble him:

. . . will it be a sufficient answer? Especially as the answer is not in fact direct, not an answer point by point to the theses previously expressed . . . but only by implication.

Logically, given the analysis of Ivan's atheism in Chapter III, Dostoyevsky's response is impeccable, i.e. it is the right *sort* of response. This, of course, still leaves open the question of whether in fact, and in detail he has heeded 'the obligations of art', 'so as not to mar artistic realism'. This will be the question tackled in the next two chapters, 'Has Dostoyevsky succeeded in his task at once literary and philosophical, of presenting "an artistic picture", "imagining a form of life"?'

To help facilitate answering this question some space was devoted to drawing up a number of criteria against which, I should want to argue, any candidate for an account of a form of life may be tested. These are, each of them, necessary criteria, though I should not argue that they are *in toto* sufficient criteria. The criteria outlined were as follows:

(i) An account of a distinctive form of life must include reference to some detectable differences in behaviour, though it must include much more than this;

(ii) There must also be discoverable coherent logical rules at work, but, as Winch argued, often the question of what is to count as coherent cannot be settled without some grasp of the point which following these rules has;

(iii) In addition to criteria for distinguishing coherence from incoherence any adequate account of a distinctive form of life must also indicate what the criteria are, within that form of life, for distinguishing between truth and falsehood, and between appearance and reality;

(iv) Such an account must also lead us to the position of being able to speak of what is and what is not compatible with this form of life, to the position where we might be able to distinguish which further developments are compatible with the traditions embodied in it and which would be destructive of these traditions;

(v) Finally appeal was made to Rhees's paper *Wittgenstein's Builders* to make the important distinction between those activities (linguistic and otherwise) which are part of a game and those which are part of a form of life. The distinction is between the two different kinds of significance (whether in the sense of 'point' or 'meaning'): the way in which a move or utterance in a game has significance, and the way in which the activities and utterances of, say, religious belief, have significance.

These five testing points must be now applied to the actual 'artistic picture' presented, and in doing so we shall find ourselves moving closer to a grasp of just what sense Dostoyevsky saw in the language and life of faith.

## NOTES

[1] Letter reprinted in J. Coulson, *Dostoyevsky, A Self-Portrait* (O.U.P., 1962). See pp. 224–5.

[2] Cf. P. Englemann, *Letters From Wittgenstein*, ed. B. F. McGuiness, trans. L. Furtmuller, pp. 27 and 80. The editor's footnote to a reference in one of the letters reads, 'Dostoyevsky's *Brothers Karamazov*, and the figure of the *Starets* (Zossima) in particular had

long been favourite subjects of Wittgenstein's meditations and conversations with his intimate friends' (Letter of 26 January 1920, p. 27).

[3] Reprinted in E. D. Klemke (ed.), *Essays on Wittgenstein*. For a rather fuller discussion of this point see my paper 'On the Idea of a Form of Life', *Religious Studies*, vol. 11, 1975.

[4] 'Understanding a Primitive Society' (American Philosophical Quarterly, vol. i, 1964), reprinted in P. Winch, *Ethics and Action* (Routledge & Kegan Paul, 1973).

[5] *Tolstoy or Dostoyevsky* (Penguin Books, 1967), p. 166. It is to Steiner that I owe the example of Tolstoy's remark about Vronsky.

[6] I have considered this example in greater detail in 'Imagination in Literature and Philosophy: A Viewpoint on Camus's *"L'Étranger"*', *British Journal of Aesthetics*, 1970.

[7] R. Rhees, *Discussions of Wittgenstein* (Routledge & Kegan Paul, 1970), p. 79.

# VII

## 'A Russian Monk'

... the representation of a truly perfect and noble man ... this is more difficult than anything else in the world ....

### I

Just as some philosophers might question the validity of the manner of Dostoyevsky's response to the atheism of Ivan, so many commentators, philosophical and literary, have found wanting the literary expression of Dostoyevsky's response—the figure of Zossima. In the previous chapter it was argued that Dostoyevsky's conception of what he was attempting in Book VI could be understood in philosophically acceptable terms. In this chapter I propose to open the discussion of whether or not the content, as distinct from the form of Dostoyevsky's response, is adequate.

Schematically there are two poles between which hostile criticism oscillates. On the one hand it could be argued that Dostoyevsky's attempt to refute the atheism of Ivan by means of his portrayal of Zossima and Alyosha was in itself a reasonable task to undertake, but, one in the execution of which Dostoyevsky nodded. Alternatively it could be argued that the attempt to present goodness, saintliness, will, from the outset, blunt the creative edge, dull the psychological insight of any writer. Either Dostoyevsky had displayed *hubris* in his attempt to present a literary Incarnation, or his increasing years had led him into the byways of sentimentality.

The critical clamour is widespread. D. A. Traversi[1] for example, comments

all the beauty of Dostoyevsky's prose cannot conceal the effect of Rakitin's comment: 'His elder stinks.'[2]

He argues that there is an 'artistic flaw' in the presentation of Alyosha, of which any sensitive reader must be conscious: Stephen

Ross[3] states unequivocally that Alyosha and Zossima are, as characters in a novel, simply not credible. They may be

beautiful representations of Gods on earth. But they are not men.[4]

Even Berdyaev,[5] we are reminded by more than one commentator, held the view that Dostoyevsky was unable to present fully his vision of the good life.

The argument of both Ross and Traversi focuses on Alyosha as much as on Zossima and a view common to both is summarized in Traversi's reference to

Complete discontinuity between his (Alyosha's) virtue and the general characteristics of the *Karamazov* world.[6]

This, if true, does indicate a serious weakness in the presentation of the Karamazov family and *ipso facto*, in Dostoyevsky's hope to answer Ivan through Zossima and Alyosha. The Karamazovs are undoubtedly of this world. There will, of course, always be a residual doubt about the adequacy of any answer to the unbelief of Ivan Karamazov, which could be construed as implying a call to monastic life. This is where the character of Alyosha is so important and is one of the reasons for paying close attention to Dostoyevsky's not incompatible claims that the answer to Ivan is to be found in Book VI *and* in the whole novel. The relation between Zossima and Alyosha, is also a crucial test of the fifth criterion outlined in the previous chapter as a test of the adequacy of a presentation of a form of life which is religious, as distinct from the presentation of a sophisticated enclosed 'game'. One of the ways in which this might most clearly be shown is in the connections established through Alyosha between the perhaps monastic-bound words and ways of Zossima, and the words and ways of the world outside: hence the importance of Zossima's instruction to Alyosha to leave the monastery and to marry.[7]

Before discussing that issue in detail, however, I wish to note one further point about critical comment on the portrayal of the good and the saintly, and then to move on to a preliminary discussion of the context of Book VI. Amongst those more sympathetic to Dostoyevsky's treatment of Alyosha and Zossima, the defence of Dostoyevsky is not always unambiguous. Eliseo Vivas considers the credibility of Myshkin and Zossima in his stimulating essay 'The Two Dimensions of Reality in *The Brothers Karamazov*'.[8] After arguing that Dostoyevsky's account of religion rests upon no easily-won fideistic assertion over against unbelief, he none the less continues.

> But it cannot be denied that none of his good or saintly characters — Sonia in *Crime and Punishment*, Myshkin, and even Zossima — is endowed with as dense and authentic a humanity as his evil characters. Dostoyevsky is as aware of this criticism, which it is not difficult to answer. The reason why they are not, is that genuine goodness and saintliness are harmonious, unassertive and hence undramatic, dull, affairs. But this is not a comment on them or on Dostoyevsky but on us, his readers.[9]

Vivas, for all his acuteness of insight on other issues, seems to want to have it both ways here. That goodness and saintliness appear undramatic and dull may well be a comment on us, for dullness and lack of dramatic excitement may be a reflection of the state of mind of the reader. But, harmoniousness and unassertiveness do not obviously to the same degree depend upon the eye of the beholder. If Zossima's life and bearing have these qualities of unassertiveness and harmoniousness, then that is in fact at least a reflection upon Dostoyevsky and his conception of goodness. Whether or not that conception of goodness must inevitably appear dull or lacking in humanity is still an open question. Vivas's pessimism on this point was not shared by Dostoyevsky although he was by no means confident of his ability to carry out the task of portraying saintliness in a way that would engage his readers.[10] He did realize, however, that if he was to answer Ivan a dull, lifeless, abstracted goodness would not do. If saintliness is an answer, it must be a saintliness that will engage the emotions as well as trace out a coherent life.

Book VI is entitled 'The Russian Monk' and our assessment of the adequacy of Dostoyevsky's portrayal of saintliness should begin there.

Zossima's biography falls into three main sections each dealing with some sort of crisis in the life of the central figure of each section. The formal link between the three is, of course, Zossima, though he hardly figures at all in the first sketch, and only in a secondary, albeit crucial, role in the third. A further and important point of unity is the appearance and reappearance of certain expressions, phrases and sentences whose sense is not immediately apparent.

The first sketch is of Zossima's brother, Markel. He is presented as possessing nothing but distaste and scorn for religion:

It was the beginning of Lent, and Markel would not fast, he was rude and laughed at it: 'That's all silly twaddle and there is no God,' he said, horrifying my mother, the servants and me too (p. 295).

There then follows the sort of tale which adorns books of piety, in which Markel falls ill and is the subject of a deathbed conversion, of a 'spiritual transformation'. In itself the tale is no better and no worse than many others of that *genre*. If it is to rise above the level of spiritual soap-opera it must do so as part of a larger pattern. The pointers to this larger pattern are to be found in the sorts of remarks which Markel began to make and in the reactions of various others to these remarks. There are raised in these remarks echoes which carry one back to Book V, and also forward to the rest of Book VI, and indeed to the whole of the rest of the novel.

Markel began to speak of life as a 'paradise' and to raise questions of his own worthiness either for the love of his friends or of the service of his servants. He insisted too that

. . . we are all in paradise, But we won't see it, if we would we should have heaven on earth the next day. (p. 296)

He also claimed, and this most puzzling of all, even to his closest relatives,

everyone of us is responsible for everyone else in every way.

His doctor gave blunt expression to what his mother suspected,

Your son cannot last long. . . . The disease is affecting his brain.

No one at the time understood what he had seen and what he was trying to say. They had, some of them, sought his conversion, but when it came it was not to a conventional or easily assimilable position. For example, to his old nurse, as she lit a lamp before the icon in his sick room, he said:

Light it, light it dear. I was a wretch to have prevented you doing it. You are praying when you light the lamp, and I am praying when I rejoice in seeing you. So we are praying to the same God (p. 296).

In this same remark we may begin to trace the outlines of one crucial aspect of Book VI, an account, alternative to Ivan's, of what it can mean to 'love life'. Certainly this is one of the features of the monk's teaching which may appear 'absurd because they are too high-flown'. To consider what he teaches here as at all intelligible is to attempt to find connections between Markel's strange remarks about nature and life in the context of what follows. Unless they can be connected with something outside of them they can only be regarded as at best paradoxical, at worst, pious and romantic non-sense.

In the narrative we are given the picture of the young Zossima growing up, impressed but not overburdened by the death and change of heart which preceded the death of his elder brother. He was brought up within a religious context but years of training in the cadet-corps erased any positive trace of that feature of his background long before he became an officer. In this section of the biography there is a second crisis and conversion: this time Zossima's own. Due to his own blind arrogance he felt himself humiliated by the marriage of a girl to a landowner who lived nearby. In due course he found opportunity to insult the other man and involve him in a duel. The duel was arranged for early next morning, and after returning home that evening 'in ugly and ferocious mood', he unleashed his venom on his batman and struck him twice on the face so that the blood began to flow, striking him, as he related, 'with brutal ferocity'.

Next morning, early awake, watching the sun rise and listening to the birds sing he found himself unable to account for a strange feeling of shame and disgrace. He was out of joint with his surroundings, and suddenly he realised the cause of it as he recalled the scene the previous night:

There he stood before me and I was slapping his face as hard as I could, and he was standing stiffly to attention, his head erect, his eyes fixed blankly on me as though on parade, shuddering at every blow but not daring to raise his hands to protect himself— and that was what a man had been brought to, that was a man beating his fellow-man! What a horrible crime!

It is this point which Dostoyevsky chooses to reintroduce the 'strange words' of Markel: at this moment Zossima begins to see what sense they may have. The context, master and servant, suggest to him Markel's question, 'Do I deserve to be waited on?' but inevitably Markel's further remarks come to mind, raising questions which had never hitherto confronted him.

Zossima looks back on this as the beginning of conversion. He tells us of then becoming aware of 'the whole truth in its full light'. The truth however, is not the truth about 'eternal questions', about questions 'unsuitable to a mind created with only three dimensions'. The whole truth of which he then becomes aware is the truth of self-knowledge which is, of course, the truth about the situation in which he finds himself, and of what brought him there:

'What was I going to do? I was going to kill a good, clever, noble man, who had done me no wrong, and by depriving his wife of happiness for the rest of her life I should be torturing and killing her too (p. 308).

In itself, however, perception of the truth was not sufficient: the situation had to be changed. It was still the case that he had ill-treated his servant: it was still the case that he was pledged to make of this intelligent, honourable man, either a corpse, or a murderer.

The crux was initially his perception of Afanasy, his servant as a fellow man with equal rights, equal status, his perception of him as a man to be respected and loved simply because he was a man, a fellow creature. To see this is to see as appropriate his subsequent action, his begging forgiveness of Afanasy for the cruelty of the previous night. This was the natural expression and accompaniment of his insight. Following this we have the account of the duel in which he allowed his opponent to fire but refused to return the shot, giving instead an apology. This was as much to the consternation and upset of his opponent and second as his apology had been to Afanasy:

Can you disgrace the regiment like this, facing your antagonist and begging his forgiveness?
Gentlemen . . . is it really so wonderful in these days to find a man who can repent of his stupidity and publicly confess his wrong-doing?
But not in a duel. . . . (p. 309)

His insight into what he took to be the true state of affairs could not be stifled by the etiquette of the situation, by a false sense of honour: the nature of his insight carrying with it the insistence that the relation between master and servant is the relationship between one man and another, and that human life is of more importance than specific beliefs about what is socially permissible, has altered his conception of both honour and integrity. He no longer connected these concepts with the formal criteria for honour and integrity laid down by the social group to which he belonged. Rather he had established in his thinking and acting, a connection between these concepts and the perception of the possibility of different relationships holding between one man and other.

The narrative of the biography then moves on towards the third main episode, reaching a dramatic height which throws into much sharper relief the features which it shares with the other two episodes.

After his apology at the duel Zossima was treated for a time as a socially fashionable eccentric; someone to be exhibited at polite gatherings; someone whose strange sayings were the latest novelty. For most, his explanations of his action were simply occasions initially for incredulity, then subsequently for good-humoured banter:

'But how can I possibly be responsible for all?' everyone would laugh in my face. 'Can I, for instance, be responsible for you?' 'You may well not know it,' I would answer, 'since the whole world has long been going on a different line, since we consider the veriest lies as truth and demand the same lies from others. Here I have for once in my life acted sincerely and, well, you all look upon me as a madman. Though you are friendly to me, yet you see, you all laugh at me.' (p. 311)

Gradually interest in this latest novelty began to wane, but amongst his listeners he noticed one face in particular which spoke of intensity and seriousness.

The man in question, visited him in his room and spoke of his admiration for Zossima's strength of character in apologizing as he had done at the duel,

. . . as you have dared to serve the truth, even when by doing so you risked incurring the contempt of all (p. 312).

The man pressed his admiration speaking in such a way as to reveal that he was carrying the weight of 'some peculiar secret in his soul'. He began to visit Zossima regularly to talk to him about his public remarks which caused alternatively consternation and amusement, and to reveal that he himself shared some of Zossima's beliefs. In one instance he elicited a strain of scepticism in Zossima and made this the occasion of extending and deepening their area of shared insight.

Speaking of Zossima's insistence that every man should be responsible for every other he argued that when men come to recognize and grasp this idea then the Kingdom of Heaven will come to be a reality. Zossima questioned bitterly, with disillusion, whether this would ever happen. The mysterious stranger assured him that it would, and began to analyse the changes which would be necessary to ensure this. He did this by showing how, in the pattern of life which both he and Zossima are concerned to see overthrown, a whole series of conceptual connections are made which lead to an analysis of certain key concepts entirely different from the one which they should like to see in its place. This is particularly so in the case of the concepts of security and self-realization.

He argued that initially what is required is 'a change of heart'. Part of what this means is seen in opposing this to 'scientific advance'. If the hope of both Zossima and himself is the realization of the Kingdom of Heaven, a sharing of all things between men, 'Then', he argued, 'this will not be brought about by any scientific advance'. Science and technology may make more resources, more goods available, but they provide no entailment about how these goods are to be distributed, how the resources are to be used. There are simply more items to be possessed, more resources to be channelled into increasing the prosperity of men. No canons have been laid down about who should possess these goods, or which men benefit from the increased prosperity. The distribution of the fruits of scientific advance must be settled independently of that advance.

A second feature of what he means by 'a change of heart' comes out in his insistence that what this will amount to is the end of 'the period of human isolation'. When asked what account he will give of this concept he argued that such isolation is a corollary of a particular interpretation of the concepts of security and self-realization. This interpretation sees security as the outcome of the acquisition of material wealth. Self-realization is seen as necessarily a solitary and exclusive business. The chief fear of such a position is that of relying in any sense upon the help of one's fellow-men. Instead, reliance is placed upon the accumulation of riches, the more they help one to gain independence of one's fellow men, the more one believes oneself to be secure:

Everywhere in these days men have, in their mockery, ceased to understand that the true security is to be found in social solidarity rather than in isolated individual effort.

The paths of isolation lead not to self-realization, but to self-destruction.

All of the above formed part of the teaching of the mysterious stranger, teaching whose exposition formed the substance of many lengthy conversations. Despite the insight, however, there was ever the suggestion that the stranger had, as yet, left something unsaid, something undone. There was still in his own life a form of isolation, a fundamental insecurity.

And then one evening, after he had been talking with great fervour for a long time, he suddenly and to my great surprise, turned pale, his face became contorted and he fixed me with a motionless stare. 'What's the matter?' I said; 'do you feel ill?'— he had just been complaining of a headache. 'I . . . do you know . . . I murdered someone.'

Zossima did not know whether to believe him, and even suspected him of madness. The stranger, however, clearly felt some sense of triumph, and spoke of his confession to Zossima as a first step, the implication being that it matched Zossima's apology to Afanasy: the public confession was still to come.

The details of the crime are important, for they help define the inner compulsion to confession as one which had neither strain of self-interest, nor appeal to consequences as a justification. No one suspected the stranger of the murder of many years before. The man who had been accused had died before the trial as a result of completely unrelated circumstances. No one else had had to suffer as a result of his crime, and indeed after these many years nothing positive, it seemed, would be accomplished by his confession. Quite to the contrary, the pain and anguish which his wife and children would have to endure would, on any conceivable calculus, outweigh the possible advantage. This example of self-imposed duty to confess would have appealed to Kant who spoke of moral duties in the following terms:

'The sublimity and inner worth of the command is the more manifest in a duty, the fewer are the subjective causes for obeying it and the more those against. . . .'[11]

There were many reasons which could be given for not moving on to public confession, and the stranger wavered between statements of resolve and going over these reasons in his own mind. He spoke of the public confession as the point at which true peace could begin, from which date 'it will be paradise for me'. As day succeeded day he battled with himself, trying to strengthen his resolve: he projected his own dissatisfaction with himself by assuming that Zossima was criticizing him, wondering each time he saw him, 'Not yet?' The crucial question was:

But is it necessary at all?

And this is one of the questions which Dostoyevsky is most concerned to raise. He gives dramatic form to it, and in so doing poses a fundamental question about the nature of moral guilt and innocence. He is too, in his own way, showing what it can mean for a man to see sense in the language of guilt, innocence, and expiation.

Zossima's advice when requested is always that he should confess:

'Go!' said I, 'confess. Everything passes, only the truth remains!
'All will understand your sacrifice', I said to him, 'if not at once, they will understand later; for you have served truth, the higher truth, not of the earth.' (p. 362)

Here again, we see the posing of fundamental questions. Is there such a thing as 'higher truth, not of this earth'? *What* sense can be given to such a notion? *How* can sense be given to such a notion? Dostoyevsky's answer to these questions is in terms of *showing what it is* to give sense to the terms involved. At one level, the stranger feels himself being goaded into action by Zossima, and this comes out most dramatically on the day on which he finally decides to go ahead and confess publicly.

That actual confession takes place during a party held by the stranger to celebrate his birthday. Inevitably it causes a sensation:

. . . everyone was amazed and horrified, everyone refused to believe it and thought that he was deranged, though all listened with intense curiosity. A few days later it was fully decided and agreed in every house that the unhappy man was mad (pp. 322–3).

He did in fact fall ill, and Zossima was soon being blamed for having unsettled his mind. He was, however, allowed to visit him once before he died. It was then that the stranger both spoke of the peace of mind which he had achieved, and also revealed the depths which he had sounded in his inner struggle. The day before the confession, when Zossima had counselled him once more to confess, he had parted from Zossima in a fury. Much later, around midnight he had returned, pretending to have forgotten something. In fact he had returned intending to kill Zossima. He could not bear the knowledge that Zossima knew:

Now, I thought, he is all that binds me, and he is my judge. I can't refuse to face my punishment to-morrow for he knows all.

It was either confession or a second murder. In fact he confessed. Later people began to believe the truth of his confession, and to question Zossima,

> But I held my tongue, and very shortly after, I left the town, and five months later by God's grace I entered upon the safe and blessed path, praising the unseen finger which had guided me so clearly to it. But I remember in my prayer to this day, the servant of God. Mihail, who suffered so greatly.

The three episodes hang together, and stand or fall together. There is a growing power in the successive presentation of Markel, the young man Zossima, and Mihail. Each leads us a further step towards seeing the sense in the 'strange words' which we hear first on the lips of Markel, then successively on the lips of the other two. Dostoyevsky's hope is that by the time we have read of Mihail's internal struggles we shall have ceased to dismiss the story of Markel, and his reported sayings as merely the milk and water of sentimental pietism.

## III

Initially there are two general comments which I wish to make upon Zossima's biography.

There is little in Book VI that would help deflect the claim that Dostoyevsky's positive conception of the good life is grounded, or perhaps 'submerged' in a mystical attachment to the notion of 'the Russian people' which renders most of what he says obscure or irrelevant. Certainly Dostoyevsky's caustic comments about European influences upon Russian culture, rendered him anathema to the Westernizers and have led many to place him squarely in the camp of the Slavophiles.[12] It would be easy to cull from Dostoyevsky's occasional writings as well as from the novels, a whole *dosier* of anti-European remarks which would seem to brand Dostoyevsky as an arch-Slavophile. His position on this issue, has however, a complex history,[13] and it is much too hasty to dismiss Dostoyevsky's remarks about 'the Russian people and its soul' as sentimental, romanticized, and reactionary. None the less much of what we find in Book VI, supports the charge of extravagant Slavophilism, from the portrayal of the peasants who briefly figure in Zossima's biography — Afanasy and the youth who was a bird-catcher — to his insistence that,

God will save his people, for Russia is great in her humility.

On this point we must clearly look beyond Book VI for elaboration of Dostoyevsky's views.

A second feature of Book VI which will require further comment is the fact that of the three dramatic conversions recounted, two of them, those of Markel and Mihail, occur shortly before death. If the account of saintliness and religious belief to be given is seriously to challenge Ivan, then that belief must be more than a matter for dramatic crises and short-lived cataclysms. The importance of Zossima and Alyosha here, is fundamental. Ivan too was prepared to quote an example of a death-bed conversion — Richard whom the good citizens of Geneva badgered into conversion in the condemned cell, and who had his head chopped off 'in brotherly fashion, because he had found grace'. Ivan rightly raises in Alyosha's mind the question not only of the morality of the Genevans in question, but also of the significance of such a change of heart. If the strange words of Markel are to help us discern a form of life which is an answer to Ivan, then they must have more significance than can be found between the death-bed and the grave, or between the condemned cell and the gallows. It is in the life of Zossima which is past, and in the life of Alyosha, much of which is yet to come, that we must look for an answer to Ivan. None the less the introduction of the possibility of religious belief initially through Markel has one advantage: the dramatic situation of a man confined to a sick-bed allows an initial emphasis to be placed on the role of language in this form of life. Markel is not in a position to underline or clarify the sense of his 'strange words' through dramatic gestures of renunciation or public confession. The language which he spoke had to carry the full weight of his belief. Just as the trivialization of the language of religion in the bar-room chatter of the Russian boys *was* the debasement of religious belief, so, conversely, at the outset of his reply, Dostoyevsky focuses our attention upon the power of language be it to confuse or to define a religious form of life.

## NOTES

[1] D. A. Traversi, 'Dostoyevsky', *The Criterion*, XVI, reprinted in *Dostoyevsky: A Collection of Critical Essays*, ed. Rene Wellek (Prentice-Hall, 1962).

[2] Op. cit., p. 169.

[3] S. D. Ross, *Literature and Philosophy* (Appleton-Century-Crofts, 1969).

[4] Op. cit., p. 154.

[5] Cf. N. Berdyaev, *Dostoyevsky* (Meridian Books), p. 206.

[6] Op. cit., p. 169.

[7] Op. cit., p. 72.

[8] From *Creation and Discovery* (Noonday Press, 1955) reprinted in Wellek, *Dostoyevsky: A Collection of Critical Essays*, and also in E. Wasiolek (ed.), *The Brothers Karamazov and The Critics* (Wadsworth, 1967). Page references are to the last of these.

[9] Op. cit., p. 67.

[10] Consider in addition to remarks already quoted, the following sentence from a letter written to his niece while he was writing *The Idiot*.

The basic idea is the representation of a truly perfect and noble man. And this is more difficult than anything else in the world, particularly nowadays.

(1st January 1868). From *Letters of Fyodor Dostoyevsky*, translated Ethel Colburn Mayne (McGraw-Hill, 1964), p. 142.

[11] *The Moral Law*, trans. H. J. Paton (Hutchinson), p. 93.

[12] For examples of writings representing each of these two perspectives see *Russian Philosophy*, ed. Edie, Scanlan and Zeldin (Quadrangle Books, 1965), vol. i.

[13] Consider as a final statement his famous 'Pushkin Address' of 1881.

# VIII

## 'A Sufficient Answer?'

And so I tremble for it in this sense: will it be a sufficient answer?

The argument of chapters VI and VII has developed two parallel themes: in Chapter VI a suggestion was offered which provides a philosophical account of how Dostoyevsky tackled the problem of giving an alternative to Ivan's insidious analysis of religious belief; in Chapter VII an outline was offered of what Dostoyevsky presents in Book VI as constituting an answer to the atheism which is a consequence of Ivan's account of religion. In this chapter I propose to apply the criteria outlined in Chapter VI to the content of Dostoyevsky's 'refutation of' Ivan. As we have seen Dostoyevsky himself raised questions about whether his answer to Ivan would be a 'sufficient answer'. My argument is that one way of testing the sufficiency of his answer will be to construe his question as a question about whether or not Dostoyevsky has successfully portrayed a form of life. This will not provide a complete answer to his question, for it is in part a literary question, but it will provide a basis from which the answers given by Traversi, Ross, and Wasiolek[1] amongst others, may be reassessed. Part of Dostoyevsky's worry about the adequacy of his response to Ivan, was at root, I suggest, a philosophical worry about whether 'an artistic picture' was a logically appropriate response. The argument of Chapter VI was that it is an appropriate type of response. If Dostoyevsky can portray a form of life in which the language of religion can play a role other than the trivial or morally unacceptable roles allowed to it by Ivan, then Dostoyevsky has refuted the implicit claim by Ivan, that there is no alternative to his analysis of religion. The question which now faces us is, 'Did Dostoyevsky succeed in portraying a form of life in which religion plays a part?'

The conception of religious belief to be found in *The Brothers*

*Karamazov* is syncretist rather than purely traditional. Certainly there are elements of traditional Orthodox piety. The use of texts and tales from Old and New Testaments, the piety of the peasants in Zossima's biography, and the setting of the monastery for a number of the central episodes in the novel, each of these points to the importance of Orthodox religion in Dostoyevsky's conception of the future. It would be a mistake, however, to assume an uncritical acceptance of 'Russian religion', lock, stock and barrel, for woven into the novel is a critique and restructuring of much that has been accepted as of the essence of religious and indeed Christian belief.

Combined with this critique of religion, to the details of which we must shortly turn, were elements of a form of nature mysticism which helped give content to those aspects of Dostoyevsky's thought hailed most enthusiastically by contemporary Slavophiles. The 'strange words' of Markel, and the illumination of the young Zossima's mind drew strongly upon the freshness and apparent innocence of natural life. Markel asked forgiveness of the birds, 'for I have sinned against you too', and he found, as did Zossima later, intimations of the presence of God in the beauty of early spring. Civilization, particularly in its industrialized forms had helped separate men and women from such sources of peace and light. It is easy to see how the deep-seated Russian belief in the importance of peasant life and religion as repositories of faith and wisdom, received firm endorsement, for were not the peasants least detached of all from the potential insights of nature.

The symbolism of 'embracing the earth', 'kissing the earth', and bowing down to touch the earth, all help to strengthen this composite of nature mysticism and peasant life, for is not the earth in question, the *Russian* earth? It is slavic soil which in almost magical fashion is invoked as a source of strength and purification. Inevitably to western minds this smacks of superstition. The embryonic forms of self-expression from which such beliefs may grow, however, are to be found in the most unexpected places. Ronald Clark tells us, for example, that upon his return to England from a spell in the diplomatic service in Paris, 'after going on his knees to kiss English soil again', the young Bertrand Russell (1894),

pencilled a note to Alys which described how he was now 'on English ground once more, my soul brimming with patriotism, enjoying bad tea & bread and butter because they are English'.[2]

Reservations cannot be wholly dismissed, but they can be tempered by a realization of the dangers of over-literal interpretation. The error of seeing only crude and naïve superstition is even more clearly indicated in the far-reaching reformulation of religious belief and beliefs which takes place throughout the course of the novel. The religious conception most closely scrutinized by Dostoyevsky is that of 'miracle', one through which superstition can become most clearly manifest.

Within the novel the concept of miracle recurs at various stages in the development of the dialectic which takes place between belief and unbelief. The Grand Inquisitor insists that with mystery and authority, belief in miracle is a desperate need of the weak, and part of 'correcting' the work of Christ is his insistence that Christ should have turned the stones into bread. The psychological desire for miracle is closely tied to the satisfaction of physical need. The cynicism of the Inquisitor, however, presupposes a rejection on his part of the naïve and superstitious acceptance of miracle by many of the faithful of the day. This is paralleled in old Karamazov's argument with Smerdyakov about whether or not faith can move mountains, and those imputing simple-minded slavophilism to Dostoyevsky should pay close heed to Karamazov's concluding comment to Smerdyakov and Ivan:

Stay. . . . So you do suppose there are two [sc. 'and they most likely are saving their souls in secret somewhere in the Egyptian desert' (Smerdyakov)] who can move mountains? Ivan, make a note of it, write it down. There you have the Russian all over (p. 131).

Earlier at the monastery Karamazov, in typical form, had enlisted on the other side of the debate, asking Zossima about the truth of a story

. . . told somewhere in the 'Lives of the Saints' of a holy saint martyred for his faith who, when his head was cut off at last, stood up, picked up his head and, courteously kissing it, walked a long way carrying it in his hands (p. 39).

Of such stuff are certain types of religious belief born.— The belief of a Madame Hohlakov, of a superstitious peasant, or of a demented monk. Zossima rejects the story out of hand, but Dostoyevsky uses the occasion for some mild satire on the approach to miracles adopted in ecclesiastical scholarship. Father Librarian, standing nearby enters the discussion with bibliographical comment and request:

There is nothing of the kind in all the lives of the saints. What saint do you say the story is told of?

There then follows a rather comical uncovering of the source of the story as the claim of a Frenchman in Paris, who allegedly had heard it read in a Russian Orthodox mass, and had later told it to Muisov, who had passed it on to old Karamazov during some dinner party or other. The section could be read as a nineteenth-century extension of Hume's discussion of the source of miracles published more than a century before in his *Enquiries*.

The stumblings of Muisov, the earnest question of Father Librarian, the reactions to other events in this section of the novel contrast starkly with Zossima's blunt 'No, it isn't true' to Karamazov's original question. These early infiltrations of the concept of miracle into the novel help prepare the ground for the role which miracle has thrust upon it as the arbiter of the authority of Zossima's faith, and of the acceptability of the claims made for his sainthood. That such a test is to be put to Zossima's religious status is made precise in the attitudes of one of the host of diverting minor characters in the novel — the monk from Obdorsk, 'a monk', the narrator tells us, 'of humble peasant class, of narrow outlook, but a true believer'. He observes all that goes on in Zossima's cell, and all the tales of wonder and alleged miracle manufactured by Madame Hohlakov and others. His natural inclinations lead him to view the fanatical Father Ferapont as the true candidate for sainthood in that particular monastery. Ferapont, an ascetic who lives the life of a recluse is the subject of rather dramatic religious experiences which as we are told always follow a period of fasting, sleeplessness and 'eating mushrooms'. But despite this, the evidence, according to the tales of miracles performed, seems to point to Zossima. Which is the true saint, Zossima who accepts gifts from some of his many visitors: Zossima who spends more time talking to those who seek his blessings, than he does in prayer and meditation: Zossima who has little time for fanaticism, for the excesses of religion; Zossima who does not encourage belief in miraculous powers, and who is accused by Ferapont of prescribing medicine as a cure for demon-possession? Or is Ferapont the true saint; Ferapont who fasts, who goes many nights without sleep; Ferapont who experiences many strange states of mind, who claims to communicate directly with God; Ferapont who believes firmly in the existence of devils, and for whom austerity is the final measure of faith?

Gradually a test of sainthood is devised in the mind of the monk, and that test has to do with supernatural powers. His allegiance will finally belong to which ever of Zossima and Ferapont most clearly have the overt signs of supernatural blessing. The ultimate focus for this gradually becomes the fate of Zossima's body following his clearly impending death. Two traditions are enunciated in the earlier books of the novel: one focuses round the belief that the body of a true saint will not be subject to post-mortem decomposition; the other centres upon a legend that the body and coffin of one making false claims to authentic belief, will be rejected by the forces for good, that the coffin might even literally 'fly out of the window', rejected by the community of saints.

Dostoyevsky firmly rejects the possibility of miracles of this sort providing 'objective proof', of a kind to be discerned by the Madame Hohlakovs of this world, who at the first hint of unusual events send off their minions, in this case Rakitin,

to keep a careful look-out and report to her by letter every half-hour or so 'everything that takes place' (p. 341).

Of course, by such outward criteria of sainthood Zossima fails, but the parody of sifting evidence and of 'speculating' about miraculous cures or prophecies, continues in merciless detail. Madame Hohlakov's daughter, Lise, is, it seems, healed because Zossima, the 'great healer' had laid hands on her.

What do you mean by healed? But she is still lying down in her chair.
But her night fears have entirely ceased ever since Thursday. (p. 48)

Thursday, we gather was three days before. Even the testimony of an 'expert witness' is called to support Madame Hohlakov's enthusiasm.

'I've called in Doctor Herzenstube. He shrugged his shoulders and said: 'I am amazed; I can make nothing of it.'

As we learn, however, whatever the situation, be it sickness or cure, Doctor Herzenstube 'can make nothing of it'. Undoubtedly David Hume's remark on this is entirely apposite:

If the spirit of religion join itself to the love of wonder, there is an end of common sense; and human testimony in these circumstances, loses all pretensions to authority.[3]

And Hume's subsequent comments on the delights of spreading news of local affairs let alone miracles, is an accurate representation of the roots of Madame Hohlakov's 'faith' in the miracles she attributes to Zossima.

At times even such a level-headed disciple as Father Paissy feels the strains of enthusiasm mounting within and in such a setting the death of Zossima is the initiation of the final stage of the test of the Elder's sainthood. So confident are some that the body will not decay that they fail to take the most elementary precautions, for example opening the windows of the room in which the body is laid out. In such an unusually stifling atmosphere putrefaction begins indecently soon after death. The vilification of Zossima proceeds forthwith, and the monk from Obdorsk concludes

Yes clearly Father Ferapont was right in his judgement yesterday (p. 346).

Zossima is not merely not a saint, but, as the precipitate decomposition of his body shows, he is clearly an emissary or servant of the powers of evil. Zossima 'stinks' and Father Ferapont comes to exorcise the cell in which the body lies.

All attempts to produce evidence for Zossima's sainthood are rejected, just as Zossima himself does nothing to encourage the belief in miracles. In his rejection of the extraordinary and the bizarre he is nearer to the homely common sense of the narrator of the story than to Ferapont. In initially drawing our attention to the importance of miracles in the tale, the narrator tells us,

I fancy that Alyosha was more of a realist than anyone. Oh! no doubt in the monastery he fully believed in miracles, but to my thinking, miracles are never a stumbling block to the realist. It is not miracles that dispose realists to belief. (pp. 20–1)

In his weary reply to an inquiry from the monk of Obdorsk, as well as in his concentration upon the needs of others rather than upon the means, supernatural or otherwise, by which these needs *should* be met, Zossima made plain his view of anxious preoccupation with miracles,

if there has been any healing it is by no power but God's will. (p. 50)

Likewise we are told that in so far as he has 'won over' the hearts of certain individuals, it was 'more by love than by miracles'.

Has the concept of miracle been jettisoned by Dostoyevsky, as the narrator seems to imply in the above remark? The answer is 'No', but the concept has certainly undergone a considerable change. Such miracles as are countenanced in the novel have to do with human capacity to love, and with human insight. The unusual powers which Zossima does exhibit can be traced to his insight into the minds and hearts of his fellow human beings. It is not surprising that he should see through the external façade of old Karamazov, or Madame Hohlakov, but his penetration of Ivan's malaise, and even more dramatically his kneeling before Dmitri certainly define him as a man with exceptional gifts. Typically Dostoyevsky warns us of the risks of reading supernatural conclusions into naturalistic premises. The only person who approximates to Zossima's insight into Dmitri's future is Rakitin 'the seminarist'. Rakitin, however, got it almost, rather than wholly correct. He believed Dmitri to be a murderer at the outset. It is not clear that Zossima did.

The supreme example of miracle in the novel is Alyosha's change of heart. The corruption of Zossima's body plunged him into deep despair which seemed certain under Rakitin's guiding hand to lead to Karamazov baseness. His acceptance of the offer of vodka from Rakitin surprised the latter and encouraged him to invite Alyosha to call on Grushenka. As the scene unfolds and we find Grushenka nestling in Alyosha's lap with her arm around his neck, it seems certain that the blushes of Alyosha the novitiate are about to achieve fulfilment in the baseness of the third Karamazov brother. It seems, we might say, as if only a miracle will save him. The miracle lies within Grushenka, the scarlet woman for whom Dmitri and old Fyodor are bidding. Upon learning of the death of Zossima her seduction turns to pity. Thus, in the symbolism of the novel, Grushenka 'gives an onion to a peasant'. She is not wholly evil, not irredeemably without the capacity for love and care. Perhaps after all the Inquisitor is wrong: perhaps freedom is not only for the strong and well nigh perfect; perhaps despite Ivan's despair there are grounds for hope. This 'miracle' blossoms into a visionary dream of the possibility of joy and gladness as Alyosha kneels before the body of Zossima.

The 'miracle' has wholly human roots and form. The description given of Grushenka's change of heart, albeit episodic, is completely naturalistic. The mystical vision which follows, a collage woven around Father Paissy's reading of the story of the miracle at the marriage feast in Cana of Galilee, is used to suggest even more strikingly the possibility of an end to the 'age of isolation', and the beginning of a period of joy and gladness. Whereas Grushenka gave to Alyosha, in the vision Zossima underlines the interdependence of human beings, one aspect of the responsibility of each for everyone else,

And you, my gentle one, you, my kind boy, you too have known how to give a famished woman an onion today. Begin your work, dear one, begin it, gentle one! (p. 377)

Visions are, of course, visions: Alyosha is simply 'beginning' and the novel gives no ground for believing that Dostoyevsky viewed the creation of an Orthodox utopia here on earth as anything other than a vision which we might use to inform our deeds and decisions.

Thus the concept of miracle undergoes change. The apparent return of the alleged arch-conservative Dostoyevsky to the naïve religion of a superstitious Orthodoxy seems indeed to be mistaken. Certainly Dostoyevsky draws upon the resources of Orthodox religion, but the implicit theology is far from traditional as our examination of the concept of miracle suggests. Dostoyevsky's picture of human beings was thoroughly realistic, at times realistic to the point of pessimism. The Grand Inquisitor is not wholly wrong, nor is Ivan, his creator. Dostoyevsky could not forget his experiences as a prisoner in Siberia, neither the inhumanity of those who had created such a penal system, nor the inhumanity of many of its victims. With such a vision of human nature, seeing the overt meanness and cruelty of Siberia lurking below the surface in Moscow and St. Petersburg, the description of 'miracle' may well come to seem appropriate to such changes of heart and unpredictable concern as one finds in Grushenka and in the boys whom Alyosha gathers around him.

The significance in the shift cannot be underestimated, particularly in the light of the many charges of reaction, theological and religious, laid against Dostoyevsky. The revolutionary nature of the move is further emphasized by the contrast between Zossima and Ferapont, an exceedingly important polarity within the ideological structure of the novel. Ferapont is presented as an embodiment of the whole tradition of saintliness within the Russian Orthodox Church. At times of stress within the history of the Church the embers of

Orthodox religion had been kept aglow, and then fanned into flames by the examples from the extensive literature on the lives of the saints, and by the living witness of the great, holy men. Voluntary acceptance of suffering and asceticism had been part of the Russian Orthodox tradition since the time of the 'Kievian' period in the tenth century. Drawing upon Byzantine and Greek sources, incarnations of sainthood were found in Princes Boris and Gleb who accepted and practised the importance of voluntary suffering, and in St. Theodosius of the caves (*sic*) whose self-mortification became definitive of Russian sainthood. In the fourteenth century St. Sergius reinvigorated the tradition of the ascetic-saint, and gave definitive form to the pattern of Orthodox monastic life. In rather dark and barbarous times the monasteries unified and preserved ideals of asceticism and spirituality. By the sixteenth century this tradition had become more and more introspective, and this, of course, had the effect of enshrining to the point of idolatry the definitions of piety and sainthood developed in cave and monastery. By the nineteenth century three hundred years of decay and revival had separated the church from issues of the day, from the lives of the educated town and city dwellers.

In this context the innovative significance of Dostoyevsky's rejection of Ferapont, and presentation of Zossima as his 'answer to all those atheistical propositions' can be seen for what it is — an attempt to reshape the Orthodox ideals in a fashion appropriate to an age of education, industrialization and revolution. That he should look at all in this direction was for many, a confession of bankruptcy, but the charge of the irrelevance of the Christian religion is a very different one from the charge of reactionary attachment to slavophile Orthodoxy, and it is, of course, a charge which Ivan puts much more forcefully than those who see only regression in the figures of Alyosha and Zossima.

There remain two general questions which must be addressed to the outline of religion given by Dostoyevsky's 'artistic picture', both of which relate to Dostoyevsky's own worry of whether or not it is 'a sufficient answer' to Ivan. The first of these questions has already in Chapter VI been structured round the question of whether Dostoyevsky presents us here with a form of life in which religion plays a part. The second which arises out of this is whether or not the version of Christianity offered by Dostoyevsky has been so emasculated that it is no longer recognizable as Christianity.

The first criterion — that a proposed form of life must include reference to detectable differences in behaviour — is clearly satisfied by Book VI. Nor of course, does this surprise us. On the whole, the behaviour which is depicted in Book VI speaks of dramatic differences, of, for example, the change in the young Zossima from beating his servant, to begging his forgiveness. But as was pointed out previously, difference in behaviour is not in itself sufficient to claim success in the portrayal of a form of life. More than this is required.

The second criterion outlined in Chapter VI was that there should be coherent logical rules at work within any proposed form of life. There are two different areas in which the question of coherence and incoherence must be raised. One such area is that of language. This relates directly to Markel's 'strange words': are there coherent rules for the use of these expressions, or are they, as Markel's doctor suggested, merely the ramblings of a fevered mind? The second area concerns that of behaviour: are there coherent rules and consistent criteria for assessing whether or not a particular act is a reasonable response to the situation, or alternatively whether it is the expression of a particular practice or a revolt against it? Again, at a different level the issue is one of whether or not one can assess the adequacy of different descriptions and explanations of what men and women do.

This helps to clarify the point which was earlier quoted from Peter Winch: that sometimes we are not in a position to determine what is to count as coherent or incoherent unless we can grasp the point of following particular activities. Many explanations of human action do in fact function precisely by indicating what the point of that action was. Indeed a number of philosophers take the view that explaining an action in terms of motives rather than causes is to indicate the point of the action rather than the psychological or physiological causal conditions of it.[4]

An example from Zossima's own biography is relevant here. When he refused to fire in the duel, his refusal could be understood in a variety of ways. His second saw the refusal within the practice of duelling and understood it as possibly an act of cowardice. His opponent at first regarded the refusal in the light of commonly accepted norms of rational behaviour:

if you did not want to fight, why did not you let me alone? (p. 309)

Zossima sees his action as an act of public confession and repentance

— in just the same way as his asking forgiveness of Afanasy was an act of repentance. His opponent came to see that there was more to it than he had first perceived, but his seconds and fellow officers were in turn outraged and puzzled. His action could only be understood as a complete breach of honour, unacceptable in an officer and a gentleman. He had disgraced the regiment by his cowardice: and yet, was it cowardice for surely if he had been moved by fear he would have apologized *before* the first shot had been fired? There seemed neither rhyme nor reason in what he did.

Interestingly a point which Ivan made much more fully is quietly underlined. When Zossima tells his fellow officers that he is resigning his commission in order to enter a monastery their outrage disappears. His act is accepted, but only in a way comparable to the fashion in which belief in God is accepted in the pub discussion. His act is accepted but not understood. He had, they thought, moved beyond the bounds of rational discussion and reasonable action, just as Ivan, with his Euclidean mind, claimed that religious belief and practice always did. The officers had however, less imagination, less intellectual penetration than Ivan, and so they tolerated what they took to be Zossima's irrationality. They laughed with and at him; they attempted to dissuade him; they pitied him, and they saw him as harmlessly eccentric rather than dangerously insane:

that explains everything, we can't judge a monk;
he had a dream the night before that he should become a monk, that's why he did it. (pp. 310–11)

Their understanding of Zossima was partial to the extent of being misguided. They do not accept that there are rules of coherence and incoherence which can carry their understanding beyond the indulgent tolerance of accepting a crank. Ivan sees further than they do. What he sees, however, is not the harmless eccentric but rather the possibility of justifying cruelty, of being indifferent to suffering, of suppressing human beings in the name of religion. What Dostoyevsky is suggesting is that contrary to the limited insight of the officers there is the possibility of understanding Zossima's refusal to fire; that Zossima is acting according to standards of coherence and incoherence which he understands and which we may discover. Contrary too, to the bleak vision of Ivan, the implication is that these rules do not lead to the inference that God is a tyrant who is responsible for the suffering of individual children. This latter point, however, has still to be established. Initially Dostoyevsky's suggestion is that there can be rules and standards of coherence which govern human behaviour other than those which are commonly accepted by any particular group or society. However, as the instance in question shows, to accept that this is so, involves grasping the point of action. The one person who did see the point in Zossima's action was the wife of his opponent, the woman who, largely unwittingly, had provoked Zossima's jealous insult to her husband.

In an age, and of a culture in which duelling is no longer a socially accepted practice, we can, more easily than Zossima's colleagues, concede the propriety of what Zossima did. But we may well lack the inclination to describe Zossima's action in religious terms. We may not be willing to talk of 'repentance', 'confession', nor to 'look around at the gifts of God'. None the less Dostoyevsky has led us one stage beyond the incomprehension of his fellow-officers even if it is only to agree to Zossima's secular judgement

Yesterday I was a fool, today I know better. (p. 309)

Whether or not he can lead us beyond this, to the stage of accepting the possibility that there could be a point to Zossima's entering the monastery, is still at issue.

At this stage it can be seen that in what Zossima did at the duel there is a consistency and coherence, even if regarded from a wholly secular viewpoint. Whether or not there is such coherence and consistency in his language and in his actions thereafter, or indeed in his own religious conception of his life, is a series of questions which cannot be answered without considering the three further criteria of the successful portrayal of a form of life.

Perhaps the most important ways in which consistency and coherence show themselves within a form of life, relate to the possibility of drawing distinctions between truth and falsehood and between appearance and reality. That such distinctions are present within a form of life is absolutely crucial. It would be a mistake to be over-demanding of the novel at this point and to expect that the text should duly list a set of criteria which together may be taken as necessary and sufficient for the proper description of a particular event as a miracle. The initial question concerns whether the form of life delineated in the novel does contain a working distinction between truly and falsely claiming that a miracle has taken place. Are there rules operating whereby certain sorts of claim to miraculous status for events are ruled out as false?

Clearly there are such rules and one of the foremost of these concerns the reliability of witnesses. The strictures introduced by Hume on this point are explicitly accepted by both Zossima and Dostoyevsky. Neither old Karamazov nor Madame Hohlakov strike the reader as providing any sort of grounds whatsoever for the belief in miracles. Their testimony fails whether judged by Hume's general criteria or whether assessed by Dostoyevsky's specific characterization. Likewise the exposé in the novel of how traditions can be built could quite easily be read as an imaginative embodiment of Hume's abstract description. To that extent at least, the criteria adopted by Hume as offering a distinction between true and false claims that an event is a miracle, are endorsed by Dostoyevsky. There is, of course, a major point of difference between Hume and Zossima, if not Hume and Dostoyevsky. In the end, Hume argues not simply that there *are* no adequate grounds for accepting this or that as an example of a miracle, he also argues by implication that there *could be* no such grounds. His argument rests upon a definition of what a miracle is:

A miracle is a violation of the laws of nature,

and upon a belief about the extent of our grasp of those laws, and the nature of the substantiation of those laws:

and as a firm and unalterable experience has established these laws, the proof against miracle, from the very nature of the fact, is as entire as any argument from experience can possibly be imagined.[5]

With this aspect of Hume's argument Zossima *is* in disagreement.

Although different in many respects, this argument from Hume shares one major characteristic with Ivan's rejection of belief in God. Both Hume and Ivan attack their respective goals by implying that the concepts in question are in some sense unintelligible. Ivan modifies this by allowing either a trivial or morally unacceptable sense to the claim that God exists: Hume argues, not directly that the concept of miracle is unintelligible, but that there is a contradiction involved in the claim that there *could be* good grounds for believing that a miracle had taken place. Just as in the broader discussion, the strategy is to show what alternative sense could be involved in claiming that God exists, so in the case of miracle, Zossima is countering Hume's position by suggesting an alternative sense to the term 'miracle'. Implicitly rejected is the definition of miracle as a violation of the laws of nature.

The first ground for this is that what is distinctive about miracles is not primarily their violation of the natural order. That an event runs contrary to the normal patterns of natural activity is not reason to regard it, religiously, as a miracle, whatever the view of the superstitious monk from Obdorsk. Secondly, the event which is offered as a paradigm of what a miracle is, does not obviously run counter to laws of nature as Hume conceives them. The event in question is the reaction of Grushenka to the news of Zossima's death, and its consequences for Alyosha's state of mind. There is a point of deep divergence here between Dostoyevsky and Hume. Whereas Hume would accept not only that the physical world is subject to natural laws but also that human behaviour is in principle at least wholly predictable,[6] Dostoyevsky would find such a belief anathema. From *Notes From the Underground* onward Dostoyevsky's novels offer example upon example of characters whose unpredictability is intended in part at least as a metaphysical assertion. It is precisely the capacity of human beings to do what is unpredictable, even capricious, which is for Dostoyevsky, the clearest statement of human freedom.

The point is that Dostoyevsky rejected determinism and in so doing laid down *one* of the conditions necessary for his account of the concept of miracle. Unpredictable human actions are possible in Dostoyevsky's world, and a certain sub-class of these wholly natural events may be regarded as religiously significant. This does not, however, amount to the acceptance of every fitful act of an underground man as a miracle. As with the expression 'I believe in God' (see chapters III–IV above) so the predication of the term 'miracle' of an event is partly at least the expression of an attitude and emotion. Grushenka's unexpected response to Alyosha's grief is marked by at least two features (a) it is morally praiseworthy, and (b) it is of spiritual significance to Alyosha. It works as a palliative to his despair, reminding him in *prima facie* unlikely circumstances that the *teaching* of Zossima was not wholly illusory. Moral regeneration even in the apparently most cynical of souls is possible. Such regeneration is radically different from the uniformity of mind and purpose which the Grand Inquisitor attempts to effect by a combinations of coercion and bribery. It is not something which, in Dostoyevsky's eyes at least, can be explained in causal terms, whether those of Rakitin's half-baked neuro-physiology or any others. It is, on the other hand, a matter for awe, for wonder, and for rejoicing: each of these states of mind much prized and commended by Zossima's elder brother, and, in due course by Zossima himself. To call the event a miracle is to give expression to these emotions, and also to mark it out as of particular moral and spiritual significance.

This account is not, of course, lacking in points of contention, nor does it leave us with an easily applicable set of criteria for what is to count as either a correct or an incorrect attribution of the term 'miracle'. None the less there is an account here which does provide grounds for the rejection of the claim of a Madame Hohlakov or an irreverent Karamazov, to have been witnesses of, or participants in, a miracle. The falsehood of Karamazov's story would be rejected on Humean grounds; the falsehood of Madame Hohlakov's partly, on these same grounds which question her reliability as a witness, but partly, not as Hume would imply because emotion is present at all, but because her claim to miraculous status for Lise's 'cure' is expressive of the wrong sort of emotions. The same would apply to the desire of those who wished to see the 'miracle' of the non-decomposition of Zossima's body. The love of wonder in question there is neither morally nor spiritually edifying. It also reduces religious belief and insight to a matter of following the most bizarre of the local conjurers.

My conclusion from this is that within the 'artistic picture' in Book VI and the form of life to which the religion of Zossima and Alyosha belongs is implicit a distinction between truth and falsehood. If certain conditions are *not* met, then the claim to have witnessed a miracle is false.

A similar argument can be constructed in relation to the distinction between appearance and reality. Not anything that religious enthusiasm claims to exist, does exist, be it Ferapont's demons, or the voices which he hears. Zossima's theology adds to the inventory of things that exist no quasi-spatio-temporal entities precluded by 'Bernardism'. What Zossima does presuppose, however, is that 'there is a higher truth, not of this world', and also that human beings can have the capacity to order their lives according to that truth. By a 'higher truth', what Zossima means is what philosophically has been referred to as a transcendent order of values. By 'transcendent' is meant here, what is independent of the demands of expediency and self-interest, whether one is talking of individuals or societies. To establish that such transcendent values do exist is no more, and no less, than to establish that it is possible to live in this way. To establish such a possibility is quite within the bounds of what can be achieved by a work of fiction, for it is to show precisely what it is like, to lead a life informed in this case by such over-riding demands for honesty, humility, charity.

The fourth criterion developed in Chapter VI was that an adequate portrayal of a form of life should leave us in a position to draw inferences about what is and what is not compatible with such a form of life. We ought, if the picture is full enough, to be able to distinguish which developments are compatible with the traditions embodied within that form of life, and which would be destructive of those traditions. Dostoyevsky's 'artistic picture' at least partially fulfils this requirement. If, for example, Zossima's faith had been vindicated as many had hoped through the unnatural preservation of his physical body, Dostoyevsky would have introduced a major incompatibility into his picture of Zossima, and of the nature of religious belief. The possibility of making such a judgement shows the applicability of the fourth criterion.

There is, however, a particular problem here which relates both to the text as we have it, and to what we know of Dostoyevsky's intentions, and at this point we begin to engage upon discussion of the fifth criterion. In the novel Zossima tells Alyosha that he must leave the monastery, marry and live in the world beyond the cloisters of a formal religious community. That such a development of the 'artistic picture' is essential for the adequacy of the version of religious belief being defined is not in dispute. Whether, however, the form of life defined in Zossima can be lived outside of a closed religious community is an open question. Zossima's own recognition of 'a higher truth' led him almost immediately to initiation into a monastic community, and the others in his biography who also saw this 'higher truth' Markel and Mihail were deprived of the need to make such a decision by illness and death. Is such a development of Zossima's teaching possible?

Dostoyevsky's intention was to write a sequel to this novel with Alyosha as the central figure carrying into the world 'the higher truth' which as even Zossima admitted is 'not of this world'. Could Alyosha survive? This is the literary version of the question about the possibility of development within the form of life. The sequel novel was not written and it is an open question whether if it had been, we should have found in the final chapter an Alyosha who while in the world, was recognizably still a disciple of Zossima. Such is the portrayal of the form of life in *The Brothers Karamazov*, that we are not in a position to draw inferences one way or the other. In this sense, the portrayal of the form of life, through his 'artistic picture' is not wholly adequate, but Dostoyevsky confesses as much in his statement of intention to write a further novel about Alyosha.

The relevance of this to the discussion of the fifth criterion is clear. If what we have is a pattern of living so circumscribed that it cannot have application in the world outside the monastery, it is doubtful that we are dealing with 'a form of life' at all. If what is said in the monastery by one monk to another, has no bearing on what is said outside the monastery by one Russian to another, then the whole language and practice of monastic life may well be little more than a sophisticated game. That there was such a possibility was clear to Dostoyevsky. The monks whom we meet are a heterogeneous lot, displayed in a spectrum stretching from Ferapont to Zossima. The life of Ferapont is, in the terms outlined 'a sophisticated game'. The practice of his type of religion outside the monastery, is not possible. Whether or not this is true of Zossima's religion, remains in the context of the novel uncertain, but at least Zossima saw the need to connect his talk of 'a higher truth', of 'the love of God', with what happens outside the life and practice of religious devotions be they individual or communal. This in itself is indicative of the critique of many of the traditions of Slavic Orthodoxy, discussed earlier in this chapter.

In fact Dostoyevsky offers alternative ways of construing the relation and extension of the ascetic and the monastic to life outside of the monastic tradition. The Grand Inquisitor took the fruits of *his* asceticism and meditation to the non-monastic world, for his initial domination of others, we are told, was derivative of a care for the weak and the many which became the reason for *his* rejection of St. Theodosius of the Caves. Zossima in embryonic fashion offers us an alternative response to the monastic tradition. The energies of his declining days are largely devoted to receiving visitors. To the distress of many of his fellow-monks his strength is reserved for the throng, rich and poor, peasant and landowner, who crowd into his cell seeking his advice, his reassurance or his benediction. This provoked many muttered protests from his more conformist brothers. 'Did he not,' it is hinted, 'accept gifts and sweetmeats?' Zossima allowed the world, and some feared, the influence of the world, into the monastery. The next stage was to send the disciple who was closest to his heart out into the world. There is little point, Dostoyevsky seems to imply, in substituting for Ferapont's 'strange words' about demons and revelations, the language of Markel's and Zossima's nature mysticism unless that language has the range and subtlety implied in Rush Rhees's remarks quoted earlier

Their uses elsewhere have to do with the point or bearing of them in what we are saying now. It is the way in which we have come to know them in other connections that decides whether it makes sense to put them together here, for instance: whether one can be substituted for another, whether they are incompatible and so forth.

My argument in this chapter has consisted of an outline by selective emphasis of the nature of religion exemplified in Zossima, and potentially in Alyosha. By the criteria offered in Chapter VI above it is 'an answer', but not a wholly sufficient answer. Its failure is insufficiency rather than simple illusion or error. It has been contended that Dostoyevsky was well aware of what was still lacking, although it is not clear that he had confidence in his ability to complete his answer to Ivan. There are other evidences in the novel of his uncertainty here, and these will be one of the three central concerns of our final chapter. One of the other issues to be raised, which will be seen to be a complementary inquiry is the question left unanswered from this chapter. If Dostoyevsky is offering a reconstruction of Orthodox Christianity is it a reconstruction which still legitimately can be called Christianity?

## NOTES

[1] Traversi and Ross, op. cit., also E. Wasiolek (ed. and trans.), *The Notebooks for The Brothers Karamazov*. See Wasiolek's introduction to the notes for Book VI (p. 89).

The writing is pallid, abstract and lacking in drama; the ideas of Father Zossima read like a list of aphorisms and risk provoking the indifference that banality leaves in its train.

[2] Ronald W. Clark, *The Life of Bertrand Russell* (Jonathan Cape and Weidenfeld & Nicolson, 1975).

³ *An Enquiry Concerning Human Understanding*, X, II, p. 117.

⁴ Cf. for example, A. Kenny, *Action, Emotion and Will* (Routledge & Kegan Paul, 1963).

⁵ D. Hume, op. cit., X, I, p. 114.

⁶ Cf. Hume, op. cit.; talking of 'the constant character of human nature', he writes

The internal principles and motives may operate in a uniform manner, notwithstanding. These seeming irregularities; in the same manner as the winds, rain, clouds, and other variations of the weather are supposed to be governed by steady principles; though not easily discovered by human sagacity and enquiry (VIII, I, p. 88).

⁷ See Chapter VI above, p. 94.

# IX

# Conclusions

## (a) *Zossima, Orthodoxy and orthodoxy*

Dostoyevsky offers us as an account of Christian belief 'an artist picture', or, as I have suggested 'a form of life'. The previous chapter has involved assessment by one set of criteria of the adequacy of this reply to Ivan. A different sort of question could arise. There is, as we have noticed, a sense in which Zossima's religion is a development of Russian Orthodoxy, although, as we have also seen, there is also a sense in which there are implicit criticisms of central elements of the Russian Orthodox tradition. What, however, of orthodoxy? Does Zossima leave us with what is recognizably a form of orthodox Christianity? It is not necessary, fortunately, to engage with the contentious detail of what counts as 'orthodox'. The canvas here is a broad one and relates most directly to the central tenets of theism, let alone Christian theism.

The preoccupation in Zossima's version of Christianity is with the inner life. Certainly the qualities of inner life which are valued are very different from those upon which Ferapont lays stress, but the emphasis does contrast markedly with those for whom belief is a matter of acceptance of outward manifestations of the activity of a personal God. A miracle is a matter of the inner change of emotion and mind, something to be greeted with wonder and awe, and which we interpret as the grace of God. There is, however, no objective confirmation, no 'sign' given which will stand as firm evidence of a miraculous intervention of God. At most, we are told 'if there has been any healing, it is by no power but God's will' (p. 50), which is certainly not an assertion of the kind of divine intervention in the affairs of men anticipated by Madame Hohlakov.

Clearly being stressed here is *one* element in the Christian and indeed New Testament tradition. As such it has advantages over that element of Christian thought which does emphasize the idea of divine intervention in the affairs of men. If God does not directly intervene on special occasions which come to be known as miracles, then we do not have the problem of trying to work out why he intervened here or there, but did not intervene to save the small child of Ivan's report, from the dogs of his landlord.

The advantages, however, have limits, for if it were simply a matter of accepting that there is no God to intervene, then we should have one view of the situation. If however, as Zossima believes, there *is* a God, then even if we accept that there will be no interventions, how is it that we can be led to see some aspects of the world as expressive of God's will? Zossima's response to this is to broaden, almost without limit, the range of aspects of the world in which we may discern the grace or will of God. Thus, he suggests that an essential and fundamental aspect of the religious life is to be appreciative of the beauty of the world, and its many creatures. 'The beauty of this world of God's and . . . the great mystery of it,' he tells us, 'bear witness to the mystery of God and continually accomplish it themselves' (p. 303). The religious life involves in its foundations an awareness of the beauty and mysteriousness of the world:

. . . what grows lives and is alive only through the feeling of its contact with other mysterious worlds. If that feeling grows weak or is destroyed in you, the heavenly growth will die away in you. Then you will be indifferent to life and even grow to hate it (p. 334).

I do not at this point want to discuss directly either the truth or the meaning of claims like these. What is relevant to the topic of this chapter, however, is to compare these and like statements from Zossima with remarks from a rather different source. In response to an interviewer's question about the place of belief in the supernatural in his life, Aldous Huxley said,

The *supernatural* is the world as it comes to us in its mystery . . . One is sometimes suddenly aware of *this bottomless mystery of existence*—sometimes *one is hit by this thing*. If you choose to call it supernatural, I mean I don't know what other sense it has . . . I mean I don't believe in mysterious beings going around arranging things . . . [1]

The first part of this strikes one as remarkably close to many of the sayings attributed to Zossima, and as Huxley is pressed further about 'a mysterious being', it is difficult to resist the belief that in fact

Zossima's religion is not substantially different from Huxley's sense of the mystery of life.

None the less in addition to reaffirming his belief 'in the profound and unfathomable mystery of life . . . which has a sort of divine quality about it. . . .' Huxley insists,

one can be a complete agnostic and a complete mystic at the same time.

His sense of the mystery of life and the beauty of the world certainly owed something, though equally certainly not everything, to his experiences under the influence of mescalin, and in his comments upon these experiences it is interesting to note some striking parallels to Zossima's 'strange words':

. . . It's an immense intensification, a transfiguration of the external world into incredible beauty and significance.
It's also beyond that kind of aesthetic experience – There may be . . . a sense of solidarity with the universe, solidarity with other people . . . Understanding of such phrases as you get in The Book of Job 'Yea, though he slay me, yet I will trust in Him'—this thing opens the door to these experiences . . . which can be of immense value to people. If they choose to make use of them. If they don't choose, well this is what the Catholics call Gratuitous Grace: it does not guarantee salvation, it isn't sufficient and it isn't necessary for salvation.

The relevance of these remarks from Huxley resides in their capacity to raise the fundamental question of whether Zossima's position is different in any important ways from that of the agnostic mystic. Zossima too quotes Job and rejoices in the beauty of the world: he talks, as does Huxley, of 'solidarity with the world' of 'solidarity with other people'.

One question which we shall not pursue here is that of whether Huxley is entitled to talk in the way that he does of solidarity with the world, and, in some way that signifies more than mere ignorance, of 'the mysteriousness of existence'. Certainly he avoids some of the excesses of the sorts of humanist 'theology' sifted thoroughly by Ronald Hepburn in his contribution to *Objections to Humanism*, [2] but whether simply a sense of 'the mysteriousness of existence' does justify the sort of acceptability of the world implied in the idea of 'solidarity', would certainly be questioned by Ivan as well as by many Christians. The main issue, however, concerns the differences, or apparent lack of them, between Zossima and Huxley.

Huxley accepts the beauty and mystery of the world while remaining wholly agnostic about God and theodicy. Zossima on the other hand, tells us that

the beauty of this world of God's and of the great mystery of it . . . bear witness to the mystery of God (p. 303).

Likewise in the process of healing he sees the grace and will of God. Is he not thus, as Ivan would ask, also committed to seeing suffering as the will of God? The difference between Huxley and Zossima can be located here. There is the *prima facie* similarity that both seem to emphasize the positive, benevolent face of the world in which we live. Yet clearly certain aspects of the world have impact on human lives which is far from benevolent. The questions which these features of the world raise for Huxley are very different from those raised for Zossima. Different sorts of theories about the physical world and about human beings' capacities for vicious, mean, and psychotic (*sic*) behaviour will have to be elucidated. Even if Zossima and other believers do have recourse to such theories, they will still have the separate problem stated with lacerating incision by Ivan: What does all this have to do with the will of God? The problems of reconciling the miseries and tragedies of human life with the beauty of the world, and with the mystery of existence are radically restructured by any attempt whatsoever to talk about this world as an expression of the will, let alone the grace of God. The radical character of this change is given quintessential statement by Ivan's characterization of all attempts at theodicy as moving no nearer a resolution of the problem—'What have the children to do with it?'—than the bar-room speculations of the Russian boys and their professors. That is to say, the distinctiveness of Zossima's beliefs as Christian beliefs, rests in considerable part upon the range of problems which they generate. But in so far as they do generate these problems they pose for the believer questions which are incredibly difficult if not impossible to resolve.

Zossima is certainly prepared to see value in suffering—one's own suffering—and his advice to those who become indignant about the evil of others and seek revenge, or who become dejected in its presence and fall into despair, is twofold,

Go at once and seek suffering for yourself, as though you were guilty of that wrong. Accept that suffering and bear it . . . and you will understand that you too are guilty. (p. 335)

Fly from that dejection children! There is only one means of salvation, then take yourself and make yourself responsible for all men's sins . . . (then) you will see at once that it is really so, and that you are to blame for everyone and for all things. (p. 333)

Here we see the force of Dostoyevsky's comment to his friend that Zossima's teaching was 'absurd, because it is so high-flown'. Even more problematic, however, is Ivan's persistence in questioning whether we have the right to forgive what men do to others. Do we have the right? Does Zossima ask Ivan to accept the suffering of innocent children as the will of God? In the end, if he does not, then as I have argued, he will find himself much closer in outlook to Huxley's agnosticism than is acceptable for orthodox Christianity. If he does ask Ivan to accept the world as the creation of God, i.e. not 'to return the ticket', then he does ask what for Ivan, as for many others, is to 'alter the facts', i.e. to release their grasp of the enormity of what is proposed.

### (b) *Zossima and Dostoyevsky*

As we have seen in extracts from his letters, there was a side of Dostoyevsky which wanted to believe that he had 'given answer' to 'all those atheistical propositions'.[3] He did claim in advance that Books V and VI would constitute the 'culminating point of the whole novel'. At that point, he hoped that the struggle between atheism and belief would resolve itself. And yet, a further six books followed. These were by no means the conclusion of this work, for already noted is his planned sequel which certainly had much to contribute to the dialogue between belief and unbelief. Can we then reasonably identify the voice of Zossima with the voice of Dostoyevsky?

I do not think that we can, and that for reasons more compelling than the above general points about the length of and possible sequel to the novel. The arguments in support of this view are of two general sorts. The first group are most clearly and convincingly deployed in Mikhail Bakhtin's now classic *Problems of Dostoevsky's Poetics*;[4] the second group are to be found scattered throughout the novel. Despite the linguistic juggernauts which Rotsel deliberately preserves in his translation, Bakhtin makes the central points of his analysis of Dostoyevsky's novels clear in his comment,

. . . the object is precisely *the act of passing the themes through many and varied voices*, it is, so to speak, the fundamental, irrescindable multivoicedness and variovoicedness of the theme.[5]

To Dostoyevsky he attributes the development of what he labels the 'polyphonic novel'. The distinguishing feature of such novels is the refusal of the author to give us a unified and in some sense 'official' or 'correct' view of the artistic world which he has created, by using the consciousness of one of his characters as the unblemished lens which reveals by contrast the distortions of the various alternative visions. To look for such an arbiter of the acceptable, if not the real, in Dostoyevsky's major novels, is to look in vain. The most unlikely characters correct the imbalances of the others. Smerdyakov has insights into Ivan's soul, and Rakitin perceives at least part of the significance of Zossima's reaction to Dmitri in a way that Alyosha, for example, does not.

The varying and unexpected insights into, and viewpoints of, one character by another is, of course, not uniquely distinctive of Dostoyevsky; but what Dostoyevsky did avoid, is a premiss which Bakhtin believed to be embedded deep in modern culture:

Faith in the self-sufficiency of a single consciousness in all spheres of ideological life is not a theory created by some thinker or other; no it is a profound structural characteristic of the ideological creativity of modern times, the determinate of its own inner and outer form.[6]

Such a presupposition clearly cannot be unconnected with the insistent attempts of Romanticism to define the nature of the heroic consciousness, though its roots go much further back than that. Bakhtin regarded this presupposition of the adequacy of the single consciousness to the representation of the ideological elements of a complex novel (let alone of a period of ideological upheaval), to have cast a blight over much cultural and intellectual life, not least his present concern of the interpretation of Dostoyevsky's novels.

Dostoyevsky he claims, and argues convincingly, neither offers a single ideological, albeit artistically complete, mouthpiece, nor does he believe that such a single viewpoint could adequately meet his ideological demands. The exploration of major ideological and metaphysical situations was for Dostoyevsky inevitably dialogical: the issues at stake could not be resolved within a single conscious and consistent outlook. It is important to stress that this assertion is quite different from the claim that human psychology and artistic realism combine to deny the authenticity of fictional characters who behave in totally and meticulously consistent fashion. Bakhtin's judgement is that Dostoyevsky could not accept any single metaphysical picture with its consequent ideology, and that this is what dominated the structure of his novels. The relevance of these general contentions to the theme of the present chapter is this: if Dostoyevsky could not rest content with an ideology expressed through the mouth of any single character, then this is as true of Zossima's view of the world as it is of Ivan's or of Raskolnikov's. There is a paradox here which doubtless Dostoyevsky would have been happy to accept. Whereas the insistence upon the importance of many voices in the pursuit of truth is doubtless partly a legacy of the Russian Orthodox doctrine of the importance of the community as the source or repository of truth, its outworking in this case is to place Ivan's voice on a footing with Alyosha's, the Inquisitor's alongside Zossima's. To reject the identification of Zossima with Dostoyevsky on these grounds however, is radically different from the dismissal of Zossima by Ross and Traversi quoted above in Chapter VII. None the less it does stand in need of, and can be given, further justification in terms of the development of plot and characterization within the novel.

As we have already noticed, Zossima's prescription for the human race outside the monastery, remains at the end of the novel still unfulfilled. Alyosha's final scene with the children is perhaps the most hopeful, but like Sonia's influence on Raskolnikov, it offers us hope rather than either promise or fulfilment. Likewise such moments of illumination and moral development as one sees in either Grushenka or Katya are temporary or at most embryonic. Their particular paths to regeneration will be long and arduous as we are informed by their all too human responses to one another in Dmitri's cell. In some ways Dmitri seems the best prospect for the influence of Zossima, but in the cells he is well aware of his capability of murdering any guard who attempts to humiliate or insult him (contrast Zossima's behaviour at the duel). He still talks also of escape and flight to America, betraying at that point little sign of a Socratic renunciation of escape, and acceptance of suffering. When he does think in terms of bearing the unjust penalties which are his fate, we encounter a most extraordinary spectacle.

In the penultimate chapter, ominously titled 'For a Moment the Lie Becomes Truth', we find Alyosha discussing with Dmitri possible plans for escape. Alyosha appeals as much to the arguments of the Inquisitor, as to the injunctions of Zossima. Dmitri considers the possibility of accepting the suffering of unjust imprisonment and exile in the hope of bringing about self-regeneration: Alyosha counsels,

Listen, you are not ready and such a cross is not for you. What's more, you don't need such a martyr's cross when you are not ready for it.

He questions explicitly the apparently unqualified faith which Zossima (and according to many commentators, allegedly Dostoyevsky) puts in the redemptive power of suffering:

You wanted to make yourself another man by suffering. I say only remember that other man always, all your life and wherever you go; and that will be enough for you.

The possibility of bribes, a mechanism used by the Grand Inquisitor, is countenanced, and the language of the Inquisitor is echoed in Alyosha's

Such heavy burdens are not for all men. (p. 807)

Perhaps, even if not a final judgement, this is Dostoyevsky's interim report on Zossima, that we are not all able to become such 'another man' but that we can remember always the form of life which he embodied. If we were to become such then perhaps we should become like the Inquisitor. In Dmitri's case this would amount to enduring his suffering, perhaps taking pride in this, then calling it 'quits' with no debt to any man, reaffirming, that is to say, the 'period of human isolation'. Perhaps the complete satisfaction of the demands of one's conscience, whether in the Inquisitor's case through the complete self-mortification and asceticism of the caves, or in Dmitri's through the acceptance of imposed suffering, is 'a burden too heavy to bear'. It does rather appear as if Dostoyevsky was still not wholly convinced that the 'God-man' was a possibility for us, any more than the attempt to become the 'man-God' could succeed for the Inquisitor.

It seems as if in this penultimate chapter, Dostoyevsky mediates his way between the Inquisitor and his Christ, between Ivan and Zossima, but he offers us the uncertain certainty of neither. All he offers is hope, freedom, and a warning.

But what of Ivan, and *his* questions. As the novel ends Ivan is on a sick bed, not wholly destroyed but torn asunder by inner tensions, by his incapacity to resolve what at the opening of the novel Zossima told him he was incapable of resolving. Yet his questions remain and Zossima does not constitute an answer to them. Dostoyevsky's earlier claim to his editor that Ivan's thesis 'the senselessness of the suffering of children' is irresistible', is not diminished in any way. A metaphysic which did diminish this would do so only at the expense of 'the facts'. On the other hand a pattern of life which moved from this to the conclusion that 'all is permitted' is equally unacceptable. No single vision could encompass all that Dostoyevsky refused to omit (and the emphasis there is deliberately negative) from his vision of the world in which he lived. The only kind of novel which would accommodate his sensibilities is the 'polyphonic' novel. And yet he was not satisfied to espouse the dualism which is certainly a metaphysical option here, nor agnosticism pure and unadulterated. These are certainly possibilities which arise out of the sorts of discussion of atheism and belief surveyed in Chapter I above. What *these* conclusions mask, however, is the extent to which atheism and belief are not simply the products of rational argument. Nor, however, are they the mere by-products or rationalizations of varying emotions. Emotions are rather, or can be, constituent parts of both atheism and belief; that emotions are not simply associates or correlations of beliefs, whether atheistic or Christian, is a lesson which a novelist is in a privileged position to teach, and others besides Dostoyevsky have done so. Dostoyevsky's distinctive insights here show us how this fact correlates with those judgements about the world, about evil, and about human freedom and potentiality, which are the irreducible constituents of particular forms of atheism and belief. He explores in particular detail the correlations between *this* emotion (anger in the case of Ivan), with *these* beliefs (the unacceptability of the suffering of small children), and shows its outworking in irony and rebellion. On the other side we see Zossima's embodiment of the beliefs in the acceptability of the world of God's creation with a love and care for all creatures, and the conjunction of these with a form of nature mysticism, worked out with an attention to detail which highlights the difficulties as well as the attractions of the form of life in question.

### (c) *Philosophy and Literature in Dostoyevsky*

The limited focus of this book has been atheism and belief in *The Brothers Karamazov*. One of the central themes running through the discussion has been the contribution of literature in the context of what for many is a predominantly philosophical debate. It has been argued that amongst philosophers there is predictably an area of dispute here. about the role of philosophy. My own inclination is to believe that philosophy has many roles to play in the discussion of atheism and belief, but I have chosen to emphasize one which is unduly neglected—'bringing belief to a consciousness of itself'. ('Belief' here, of course, is used in a sense which includes as one of its varieties, rather than in a sense which contrasts with, atheism.) Within this understanding of the role of philosophy literature has a considerable part to play. Three aspect of this have been examined in relation to *The Brothers Karamazov*: in chapters II–V the elucidation of the nature of atheism was discussed; in Chapter VI conclusions were drawn, about the nature of the argument between belief and atheism rather different from those outlined in Chapter I; finally in chapters VII and VIII the nature of belief portrayed in the novel was examined in the light of the formalisation of principles of method, given in Chapter VI. In this concluding section of the final chapter I wish to draw attention to some general points about the type of contribution which we have found this novel making to the clarification of the difference between atheism and belief.

Initially, because it is a novel, and because of many of the features of fiction stressed by philosophers, it reminds us that there are many forms of atheism and many forms of belief. It reminds us also that the separation of the accidental features of the atheism or belief of individual characters from the essential features, is both important and sometimes difficult. The complexity of what constitutes even one form of atheism or belief is something that lends itself to the details of literary creation. Granted these general points two of the most interesting areas of enquiry prompted by the novel are (1) the importance of the emotions in the definition of what can count as atheism and what can count as religious belief; and (2) the applicability of an adaptation of Wittgenstein's notion of 'a form of life' to the philosophical discussion of a novel. These two issues will be the concern of the rest of this section.

Ivan refuses to alter or falsify the facts. Children suffer in the most horrifying ways and any theory which does less than full justice to this is unacceptable. What is it precisely that Ivan fears? What he fears is not inevitably a denial by theodicy of the fact that people or children suffer. Indeed theodicy recognizes *precisely* this fact by its very existence as theodicy. Certainly there have been some forms of theodicy which attempt to deny the reality of evil, and some views of the world which deny the reality of pain and suffering. Ivan's protest however is not directed towards such *prima facie* implausibilities. His argument is with those views, hypotheses, speculations which basically argue, 'Yes, there is pain and suffering in this world, but . . .' What in the end Ivan refuses to accept is any diminution, any questioning of the authenticity or appropriateness of the emotions which he feels in contemplation of his catalogue of atrocities. His atheism has as one element the response of his emotions to what he sees in the world, to the facts which he refuses to deny. To alter his emotions, to question their significance would be to reclassify or redescribe the situation facing him, and would in that sense be to 'alter the facts'. This is precisely what he believes is asked of him by Christian theism.

What theodicy offers is not simply a theory which extends one's intellectual grasp of the world in which one lives: what theodicy offers is also a new set of emotions or emotional responses to that world. Now the tracing out of these different sets of emotional responses, of Ivan, and of a Christian believer, is a task particularly well-suited to a work of fiction. What gives a novel more than passing philosophical interest or capacity to divert is the extent to which this elucidation of the various complexes of emotions and beliefs has form or structure. My argument is that there is form or structure here requiring clarification, and that what makes an atheist an atheist, or a believer a believer has in many cases as much to do with the pattern of emotions which we see in his response to the world as it has to do with a formalized system of beliefs. (The word 'makes' in the previous sentence is not used in exclusively 'causal' terms, but rather in the sense of 'is distinctive and constitutive of'. Further, I am not denying the crucial importance of systems of beliefs in the description of atheism and Christian theism.)

What Dostoyevsky demonstrates in the case of Ivan is *both* that his atheism involves anger and bitterness *and* that it involves much more than this. Ivan's atheism is in the process of development throughout the course of the novel, and Dostoyevsky shows us how it is crucial for Ivan's survival that the emotions whose authenticity he refuses to deny must become part of a wider pattern of responses, emotional and intellectual, to the world about him. The particular pattern which takes outline form is that of 'rebellion'. The difference between rebellion and anger is in part a difference of complexity. Rebellion includes anger but it includes much more. It is an attempt to be coherent in one's dealings with one's fellows and in one's reactions to one's environment. It implies, as Camus has argued in both *The Myth of Sisyphus* and *The Rebel*, some values, some scale or order of importance. Whether as Ivan himself asks, one can 'live by it' is a question not answered in any general way in the novel, whatever happens to Ivan. It is a question which as we have seen, much exercised both Simone Weil and Albert Camus more than half a century later. It is a question, as we learned through Ivan's development, of the transformation of what we might call primary or immediate emotions into coherent complexes of emotion and belief. For Ivan, for his type of atheism, the preservation of the primacy of his response of anger is a condition of the acceptability of the whole complex and of individual aspects of it.

Dostoyevsky's response to Ivan which he gave us in the life and character of Zossima, and, to some extent Alyosha, emphasizes these features of Ivan's atheism by the actual method adopted to respond to them. He offered, in the end, what I have called 'a form of life', what Ivan and what Zossima exhibited but also withheld from Alyosha by telling him to leave the monastery. The creation of 'an artistic picture', or a form of life, is partly an attempt to delineate the structures of a coherence of emotion and belief. The attempt to exhibit in one's life the 'form', in question is the attempt to integrate one's responses to the world and to one's fellow human beings into a single whole. To talk here of framework and structure is not necessarily to talk of what is rigid and lacking in humanity, but it is to talk of a unity of outlook, of a congruence of beliefs and emotions, and in the end, of perhaps unformulated rules, but rules none the less which define some actions as inconsistent, and certain emotional responses as unacceptable.

The points which ought to be stressed here both relate to the emotions. First, the idea of a form of life includes on this account the idea of reconciling both beliefs to emotions, and emotions to one another. It is an error of certain types of empiricism, particular positivistic versions, to regard emotions as wholly beyond the range of rational evaluation and assessment. My suggestion is that there is, or can be, a logic of the emotions. Such a logic is one which raises questions of the reasonability of certain emotional responses, and of consistency of particular emotions within complexes of emotion and belief. As Hume pointed out, to feel proud of someone implies beliefs about the relationship between that person and oneself. If one has no such beliefs, one has misclassified the emotion. Likewise there is an inconsistency between the claims that one feels proud of someone or something and that one sees nothing of value in that person or thing. Fairly obvious points such as these, are indicative of the much more complex sorts of relationships between emotions, beliefs and values which, I am arguing, can be most successfully elucidated in a work of fiction.

Secondly the idea of a form of life is of a structure within which one can trace out the progress of emotional development which brings to what are sometimes misleadingly called 'primitive instincts', the possibility of refinement and sophistication. Relevant examples from the novel have already been discussed in other contexts: Ivan's anger and the possibility of its incorporation into something one can 'live by' in such a way that the legitimacy of the original response is not denied. Again, the novel pays close attention to the question of the form which love for others may take. Very closely questioned is the idea that love for others is easy or simple. The Inquisitor, we gather, began with a concern for others, and Christ's teaching is definitive for the Christian of what such concern is like. Yet, as anger can develop in a variety of different directions, so too can love, and the Inquisitor and Zossima each represents polarized developments of this one elementary human response to the needs of another. It is not simply, as in fourth-rate sermonizing that the one lacks the strength of will upon which the other draws: it is rather a matter of the form of life in which, in each case, a concern for others becomes embedded, and thus helps to define. The articulation of a theory of the emotions may well be the proper subject of a philosophical treatise, but the fine discriminations required in giving an account of the role of particular emotions in particular areas of life is clearly one of the important functions of literature. Where the two intersect most forcefully is in the clarification of issues such as the place of the emotions in the definition respectively of atheism and Christianity. In this as in all else to which he gave his creative attention, Dostoyevsky's contribution is pre-eminent.

## NOTES

[1] From an interview which Huxley gave on BBC Television in 1961, reported in *Aldous Huxley: A Biography*, by Sybille Bedford (Alfred A. Knopf and Harper & Row, 1974). See particularly pp. 734–41.

[2] 'A Critique of Humanist Theology' in *Objections to Humanism*, ed. H. J. Blackham (Pelican Books, 1965).

[3] See Chapter VI above.

[4] Trans. R. W. Rotsel from the Russian edition of 1963 (published Ardis Press U.S.A., 1973).

[5] Op. cit., p. 226.

[6] Op. cit., p. 66.

# Bibliography

## Works by Dostoyevsky

1 *The Brothers Karamazov*, trans. Constance Garnet, Heinemann, 1912.
2 *The Brothers Karamazov*, trans. D. Magarshack, Penguin, 1958.
3 E. Wasiolek (ed. and trans.), *The Notebooks for The Brothers Karamazov*, University of Chicago Press, 1971.
4 *The Diary of a Writer* (2 vols.), edited and translated Boris Brasol, Cassell, 1949.
5 J. Coulson, *Dostoyevsky: A Self-Portrait*, O.U.P., 1962.
6 E. Colburn Mayne (trans.), *Letters of Fyodor Dostoyevsky*, McGraw-Hill, 1964.

## Works wholly or partially on Dostoyevsky

7 T. J. J. Altizer and W. Hamilton, *Radical Theology and The Death of God*, Pelican, 1968.
8 M. Bakhtin, *Problems of Dostoevsky's Poetics*, trans. R. W. Rotsel, Ardis Press, 1973.
9 N. Berdyaev, *Dostoevsky*, Meridian Books, 1957.
10 A. Camus, *The Rebel*, trans. A. Bower, Penguin, 1962.
11 Edie, Scanlan and Zeldin (eds.), *Russian Philosophy* (3 vols.), Quadrangle Books, 1965.
12 R. Guardini, 'The Legend of the Grand Inquisitor', *Cross Currents*, vol. iii, 1952.
13 R. Hingely, *The Undiscovered Dostoyevsky*, Hamish Hamilton, 1962.
14 R. Mochulsky, *Dostoyevsky*, Princeton University Press, 1967.
15 R. Peace, *Dostoyevsky,* Cambridge U.P., 1971.
16 P. Rahv, 'The Sources and Significance of The Legend of the Grand Inquisitor', Reprinted in *Wasiolek* (24).
17 P. Ramsey, *Nine Modern Moralists*, Prentice-Hall, 1962.

18   S. D. Ross, *Literature and Philosophy*, Appleton-Century-Crofts, 1969.
19   V. Rozanov, *The Legend of the Grand Inquisitor*, Cornell U. P., 1972.
20   E. J. Simmons, *Introduction to Russian Realism*, Indiana U.P., 1967.
21   G. Steiner, *Tolstoy or Dostoyevsky*, Penguin, 1967.
22   D. Traversi, 'Dostoyevsky', in *Wellek* (25).
23   E. Vivas, 'Two Dimensions of Reality in *The Brothers Karamazov*', in *Wasiolek* (24).
24   E. Wasiolek (ed.), *The Brothers Karamazov and the Critics*, Wadsworth, 1967.
25   R. Wellek (ed.), *Dostoyevsky: A Collection of Critical Essays*, Prentice-Hall, 1962.


*Other Works*


26   A. J. Ayer, *Language, Truth and Logic*, Second Edition, Gollancz, 1946.
27   K. Barth. *The Epistle to the Romans*, trans. E. Hoskyns, O.U.P., 1933.
28   E. Bedford, 'Emotions', in *V. C. Chappell.*
29   Sybille Bedford, *Aldous Huxley: A Biography*, A. A. Knopf and Harper & Row, 1974.
30   H. J. Blackham (ed.), *Objections to Humanism*, Penguin, 1965.
31   *Book of Acts.*
32   R. B. Braithwaite, *An Empiricist's View of the Nature of Religious Belief*, C.U.P., 1955. Reprinted in *Hick* (53).
33   A. Camus, *The Myth of Sisyphus*, Vintage Books, Random House, 1955.
34   A. Camus, *The Outsider*, Penguin Books, 1961.
35   V. C. Chappell (ed.), *The Philosophy of Mind*, Prentice-Hall, 1962.
36   R. W. Clark, *The Life of Bertrand Russell*, Jonathan Cape and Weidenfeld & Nicolson, 1975.
37   J. Edwards, *The Nature of the Religious Affections*, Yale U.P., 1959.
38   E. W. Trueman Dicken. *The Crucible of Love*, Darton, Longman & Todd, 1963.
39   P. Engleman, *Letters from Wittgenstein*, ed. B. F. McGuiness, Blackwell, 1967.

40 F. Ferré, *Language, Logic and God*. Eyre & Spottiswoode, 1962.

41 J. N. D. Findlay, 'Can God's Existence Be Disproved?', *Mind*, vol. lvii, 1948.

42 A. Flew, *God and Philosophy*, Hutchinson, 1966.

43 A. Flew and A. MacIntyre, *New Essays in Philosophical Theology*, S.C.M. Press, 1955.

44 A. Flew, R. M. Hare, B. Mitchell and I. Crombie, 'Theology and Falsification', in *Flew and MacIntyre* (43).

45 S. Hampshire, 'Identification and Existence', in *Lewis* (65).

46 R. S. Heimbeck, *Theology and Meaning*, George Allen & Unwin, 1969.

47 P. Helm, 'Problems of Evil', *Sophia*, vol. v, 1965.

48 R. W. Hepburn, *Christianity and Paradox*, Watts, 1958.

49 R. W. Hepburn, 'A Critique of Humanist Theology', in *Blackham* (30).

50 J. Hick, *The Philosophy of Religion*, Prentice-Hall, 1963.

51 J. Hick, 'Theology and Verification', reprinted in *Hick* (53).

52 J. Hick, 'Theology's Central Problem', University of Birmingham, 1967.

53 J. Hick (ed.), *The Existence of God*, Collier-Macmillan, 1964.

54 J. Hick (ed.), *Faith and the Philosophers*, Macmillan, 1964.

55 D. Hume, *Dialogues Concerning Natural Religion*, ed. N. K. Smith, Nelson, 1947.

56 D. Hume, *An Enquiry Concerning Human Understanding*, Oxford U.P., 1902.

57 J. F. M. Hunter, '"Forms of Life" in Wittgenstein's *Philosophical Investigations*', reprinted in *Klemke* (64).

58 O. R. Jones (ed.), *The Private Language Argument*, Macmillan, 1967.

59 I. Kant, *The Moral Law*, ed. and trans. H. J. Paton, Hutchinson, 1956.

60 A. Kenny, *Action, Emotion and Will*, Routledge & Kegan Paul, 1963.

61 A. Kenny, 'Necessary Being', *Sophia*, vol. i, 1962.

62 A. Kenny, 'God and Necessity', in *Williams and Montefiore* (96).

63 S. Kierkegaard, *Sickness Unto Death*, Anchor Books, 1954.

64 E. D. Klemke (ed.), *Essays on Wittgenstein*, University of Illinois Press, 1971.

65 H. D. Lewis (ed.), *Contemporary British Philosophy*, Third Series, George Allen & Unwin, 1956.

66 T. McPherson, *The Philosophy of Religion*, Van Nostrand, 1965.

67 T. McPherson, 'Religion as the Inexpressible', in *Flew and MacIntyre* (43).

68 N. Malcolm, 'Anselm's Ontological Arguments', Reprinted in *Hick* (53).

69 N. Malcolm, 'Is it a Religious Belief that God exists?', in *Hick* (54).

70 C. B. Martin, *Religious Belief*, Cornell U.P., 1959.

71 A. Maslow, *Religious Values and Peak Experiences*, Viking Press, 1970.

72 W. I. Matson, *The Existence of God*, Cornell U.P., 1965.

73 J. S. Mill, *Three Essays on Religion*, Longmans, 1874.

74 T. R. Miles, *Religion and the Scientific Outlook*, George Allen & Unwin, 1959.

75 G. E. Moore, *Principia Ethica*, C.U.P., 1903.

76 D. Z. Phillips, *The Concept of Prayer*, Routledge & Kegan Paul, 1965.

77 D. Z. Phillips, *Faith and Philosophical Enquiry*, Routledge & Kegan Paul, 1970.

78 D. Z. Phillips, 'Faith, Scepticism and Religious Understanding', in *Phillips* (77).

79 A. Plantinga, *God and Other Minds*, Cornell U.P., 1967.

80 I. T. Ramsey (ed.), *Christian Ethics and Contemporary Philosophy*, S.C.M. Press, 1966.

81 R. Rhees, 'Wittgenstein's Builders', Reprinted in *Discussions of Wittgenstein*, Routledge & Kegan Paul, 1970.

82 J. Schofield, D. M. MacKinnon, I. T. Ramsey, Comments on Braithwaite in *I. T. Ramsey* (ed.) (80).

83 N. Smart, *Philosophers and Religious Truth*, S.C.M. Press, 1964.

84 N. Smart (ed.), *Historical Selections in the Philosophy of Religion*, S.C.M. Press, 1962.

85 N. K. Smith, *The Credibility of Divine Existence*, Macmillan.

86 C. L. Stevenson, 'The Emotive Meaning of Ethical Terms', *Mind*, vol. xlvi, 1937.

87 C. L. Stevenson, *Ethics and Language*, Yale U.P., 1944.

88 S. R. Sutherland, 'Imagination in Philosophy and Literature', *British Journal of Aesthetics*, vol. 10, 1970.

89 S. R. Sutherland, 'On the Idea of a Form of Life', *Religious Studies*, vol. 11, 1975.

90 F. R. Tennant, *Philosophical Theology* (2 vols.), C.U.P.,1968.

91 P. Tillich, *Systematic Theology*, vol. i, Nisbet, 1953.

92 J. O. Urmson, *Philosophical Analysis*, Oxford U.P., 1956.

93 J. O. Urmson, *The Emotive Theory of Ethics*, Oxford U.P., 1968.

94 S. Weil, *Notebooks*, vol. i, trans. Arthur Wills, Routledge & Kegan Paul, 1956.

95 B. A. O. Williams, 'Tertullian's Paradox', Reprinted in *Flew and MacIntyre* (43).

96 B. A. O. Williams and A. Montefiore, *British Analytical Philosophy*, Routledge & Kegan Paul, 1966.

97 J. Cook Wilson, 'The Existence of God', Reprinted in *Smart* (84).

98 P. Winch, 'Understanding a Primitive Society', Reprinted in *Ethics and Action*, Routledge & Kegan Paul, 1973.

99 L. Wittgenstein, *Lectures and Conversations*, Blackwell, 1966.

100 L. Wittgenstein, *Philosophical Investigations*, Blackwell, 1953.

101 L. Wittgenstein, *Zettel*, Blackwell, 1967.

# Index